Family Bible Study

THE

Herschel

HOBBS

COMMENTARY

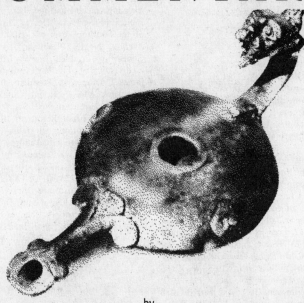

by

Robert J. Dean

SPRING 2001
Volume 1, Number 3

ROSS H. McLAREN
Biblical Studies Specialist

Carolyn Gregory
Production Specialist

Stephen Smith
Graphic Designer

Frankie Churchwell
Carla Dickerson
Technical Specialists

Send questions/comments to
  Ross H. McLaren, editor
  127 9th Ave., North
  Nashville, TN 37234-0175
  Email: HHobbsComm@lifeway.com

Management Personnel

David Briscoe, *Manager*
Adult Biblical Studies Section
Rick Edwards, *Director*
Adult Sunday School Ministry Department
Louis B. Hanks, *Associate Director*
Sunday School Group
BILL L. TAYLOR, *Director*
Sunday School Group

The Herschel Hobbs Commentary (ISSN 0191-4219), *Family Bible Study*, is published quarterly for adult teachers and members using the Family Bible Study Series by LifeWay Christian Resources of the Southern Baptist Convention, 127 Ninth Avenue, North, Nashville, Tennessee 37234, Gene Mims, President, LifeWay Church Resources, a division of LifeWay Christian Resources; James T. Draper, Jr., President, and Ted Warren, Executive Vice-President, LifeWay Christian Resources. Printed in the U.S.A. © Copyright 2000 LifeWay Christian Resources of the Southern Baptist Convention. All rights reserved. Single subscription to individual address, $20.88 per year. If you need help with an order, WRITE Customer Service Center, 127 Ninth Avenue, North, Nashville, TN 37234-0113; FAX (615) 251-5933; EMAIL to Customer Service@lifeway.com; ONLINE at www.lifeway.com; or PHONE 1-800-458-2772. Mail address changes to *The Herschel Hobbs Commentary, Family Bible Study,* Customer Service Center, 127 Ninth Avenue, North, Nashville, TN 37234-0113.

Dedicated to

Billy Graham,

who for over 50 years

has preached the good news of salvation in Christ

to millions of people all over the world.

Contents

Study Theme

One Solitary Life: The Life Of Jesus

Contents

Study Theme

One Solitary Life: The Life Of Jesus

Unit 4: No One Else Like Jesus

On one occasion the enemies of Jesus sent temple guards to arrest Him (John 7:32). When they arrived where Jesus was teaching in the temple, they began to push through the crowds. At some point, they stopped and listened to what Jesus was saying. They heard Him say, "If anyone is thirsty, let him come to me and drink" (v. 37, NIV). They did not arrest Jesus. When the guards returned without Jesus, their superiors asked them why they had not brought Jesus as ordered. They replied, "No one ever spoke the way this man does" (v. 46, NIV).

We could say the same thing about every aspect of the life of Jesus. For example, we could say: "No one ever was born the way this man was born. No one ever lived as this man lived. No one ever died the way this man died. No one ever was raised from the dead the way this man was raised. No one can save except this man." There truly was and is no one else like Jesus. In one of his best moments, Simon Peter said, "Lord, to whom shall we go? thou hast the words of eternal life" (6:68).

This four-session unit of study examines teachings and miracles from Jesus' Galilean ministry. These lessons focus on Jesus' forgiveness and healing of a paralyzed man who was brought to Him by four men, Jesus' teaching concerning loving enemies, Jesus' calming a storm at sea and healing a demon-possessed man, and Jesus' feeding of the five thousand.

The Life Impacts of these sessions are designed to help you:
- bring others to Jesus through your words and actions (Mar. 4).
- act in love toward those who mistreat you (Mar. 11).
- depend on the compassionate Christ (Mar. 18).
- make yourself, and all you have, available for service to Christ (Mar. 25).

Do you believe there is no one else like Jesus? _____
What would you cite to someone as proof of Jesus' uniqueness? _____
Why is it important that Jesus is unique? _____

BRINGING OTHERS TO JESUS

Bible Passage: Mark 2:1-12
Key Verse: Mark 2:5

❖ *Significance of the Lesson*

• The *Theme* of this lesson is Jesus is the only One who can forgive sin.
• The *Life Question* this lesson seeks to address is Do I really believe there is no one else like Jesus?
• The *Biblical Truth* is that believers demonstrate their faith that there is no one else like Jesus by bringing others to Him.
• The *Life Impact* is to help you bring others to Jesus through your words and actions.

Coming to Jesus and Bringing Others to Him

Many adults struggle with the idea that they and others need what only Jesus can give. Some are not convinced that Jesus is the only Savior. Some refuse to admit their need. Some who have come to Jesus are reluctant to bring others to Him. They are reluctant to share their witness for various reasons, including fear and lack of conviction.

The biblical worldview affirms the universal need to come to Jesus for forgiveness and new life. Those who find in Him the answer to their greatest needs have the obligation to bring others to Him.

Sickness and Sin, Forgiveness and Health

What is the relationship between sin and sickness? A variety of answers are given. Some feel that sickness is the direct result of the sick person's sins. This was the view of Job's three friends, as expressed by Eliphaz in Job 4:7. It also was the view of the apostles in John 9:1-2. The Book of Job shows that the three friends were wrong (Job 42:7-10). Jesus told the disciples that the man born blind was not being punished for his sins (John 9:3-4). On the other hand, sickness sometimes is the result of sin. This seems to have been true of the man in John 5:1-14 (see v. 14). Many infer from Mark 2:5 that this was also true of the sick man in this lesson. James 5:14-16 teaches that sickness is always an occasion for confessing our sins and being forgiven—whether or not sin was the direct cause of the sickness.

Forgiveness of sins does not always lead to restored physical health, but being right with God is essential for a person's total well-being. Paul's thorn in the flesh was never blamed on some sin, and it was not taken away when he prayed; however, God taught him important lessons for life from his experience with pain (2 Cor. 12:7-10).

Son of Man

Mark 2:10 is the first time in Mark's Gospel the title "Son of man" appears. This is the favorite title Jesus used when speaking of Himself. It appears 84 times in the Gospels and all but one of these is spoken of Jesus concerning Himself. In the Old Testament, these words generally refer to a man. However, Daniel 7:13 is a vision of the future divine Son of man, who would receive the eternal kingdom. Jesus chose to use this title and avoid other titles, about which the people had false ideas. Jesus' use of this title can be grouped in three ways: of His earthly ministry (Mark 2:10,28); of His suffering, death, and resurrection (8:31); and of His return (v. 38). The title affirms both the humanity and the deity of Jesus, but shows that He would suffer and die to fulfill His mission.

Word Study: *Forgive, Forgiven*

The Greek word *aphiemi* has many meanings, although all of these have the basic meaning of letting something go. The word can mean "let go," "send away," "divorce," "leave," "give up," "abandon," "tolerate," "forgive," "remit," "cancel," or "pardon." The last four meanings relate to sins. Forgiving sin thus means to send or take away sin, to remove it as a barrier to a relationship, to pardon or cancel any debt one owes to the one forgiving. This is the word used for forgiveness in verses 5,7,9, and 10 of our lesson. When God forgives sin, He pardons our guilt and removes sin as a barrier to our relationship with Him.

❖ *Search the Scriptures*

When many people crowded in and around the house where Jesus was, He spoke the word to them. When four men came with a paralyzed man, they showed their faith by finding a way to get the man before Jesus. The Lord forgave the man his sins when He saw their faith. When the scribes thought this was blasphemy, Jesus asked whether it was easier to tell someone his sins were forgiven or to heal him. To show that He as Son of man had the authority to forgive sins, Jesus healed the paralytic. When the man rose and walked, the crowd marveled at what Jesus had done.

In analyzing such an account, it is well to begin by noting when it happened, where it happened, and the people involved in the account. The people involved in verses 1-12 were the crowds, Jesus, the sick man, the four who brought him to Jesus, and the scribes. As we study this lesson, we seek answers to questions such as these: What do these verses reveal about Jesus? about sickness and disability? about faith? about sin? about forgiveness? about unbelief? about God? The primary focus in this lesson is on bringing others to Jesus. This incident is described also in Matthew 9:1-8 and Luke 5:17-26. In this lesson we will see the friends' determination to bring their friend to Jesus, the religious leaders' antagonism to Jesus, and Jesus' authority to heal and forgive.

The Friends' Determination (Mark 2:1-5)

How did Jesus respond when crowds invaded His privacy or interrupted His preaching? How did the four men show their faith? Did the sick man have faith? Why did Jesus forgive the man before He healed him? What, if any, was the relationship between the man's illness and his sin? These questions are addressed in comments on verses 1-5.

Verses 1-2: **And again he entered into Capernaum after some days; and it was noised that he was in the house. ²And straightway many were gathered together, insomuch that there was no room to receive them, no, not so much as about the door: and he preached the word unto them.**

When and where did this incident happen? Review Mark 1:21-38, which tells of Jesus' earlier ministry in Capernaum. Verses 39-45 tell of a ministry in other parts of Galilee. In 2:1 **again** refers to Jesus' return to **Capernaum.** Matthew 9:1 says that He "came into his own city."

In the house shows where Jesus was in Capernaum. Jesus had made this seaside city His base of operations in Galilee (Matt. 4:13). Some translations, such as the *Holman Christian Standard Bible,* have "at home" (HCSB, NASB, NRSV, REB) rather than **in the house** for *en oiko.* The *New International Version* agrees with this and reads, "he had come home." Some Bible students think that Jesus had His own house in Capernaum. But we know that Simon and Andrew had a house in Capernaum (Mark 1:29), and Jesus probably stayed in their house when He was in town. After all, Jesus later told a would-be follower, "Foxes have holes, and birds of the air have nests; but the Son of man hath not where to lay his head" (Luke 9:58). We conclude that just as Jesus made Capernaum the base city for His ministry, so did He make the home of His two disciples His temporary residence while there.

After some days is not specific, but it implies that Jesus' ministry in 1:39-45 was several days. It could have been only "a few days" (NIV); it could have been several weeks. **After some days** modifies **entered,** not **noised** ("heard," NIV). It was not several days before the people heard that Jesus was in the house in Capernaum. **Straightway** is not in the best Greek texts, but the idea is present. Soon after Jesus returned, **many were gathered together.** So many people came to the house that **there was no room to receive them, no, not so much as about the door.** The crowd filled up the inside of the house and spilled out onto the street.

Notice how Jesus responded. He did not complain about having no privacy. Instead, He seized the opportunity and **preached** ("was speaking," NRSV, HCSB, NASB) **the word unto them.** Followers of Jesus should follow His example. What was His theme? Mark 1:14-15 gives a summary of His preaching during those days.

Tom and Gloria Thurman, International Mission Board missionaries to Bangladesh, learned this lesson. They have an "open-door" policy. All visitors—Christian, Hindu, or Muslim—are welcome to their unlocked home. And visitors come at all hours of the day and into the night—for advice, for help, or just to talk. In their early days as missionaries, they savored a quiet time together in the morning to drink their coffee. One morning a visitor came. "I was annoyed that we hadn't even gotten to finish our devotional," recalls Gloria. "Then I got to thinking. Those men had left their homes about 4:30 that morning to walk there, and they were going to walk back home and work in the field. The Lord used that to help me see that it's not always 'my time.'"

Verses 3-5: **And they come unto him, bringing one sick of the palsy, which was borne of four. ⁴And when they could not come nigh unto him for the press, they uncovered the roof where he was: and when they had broken it up, they let down the bed wherein the sick of the palsy lay. ⁵When Jesus saw their faith, he said unto the sick of the palsy, Son, thy sins be forgiven thee.**

While Jesus was speaking to the crowd, something happened that most speakers would have resented as an intrusion or interruption. While Jesus was speaking, parts of the roof began to fall in front of where He was. Since the people were packed in, this debris no doubt began to fall on some of them. Something was happening on the flat roof of the house. Jesus saw the faces of men looking through the large hole in the roof. Then a bed was slowly lowered in front of Jesus. On it was a man who was unable to walk. Verses 3-4 tell us what had happened.

The man on the bed was **sick of the palsy** ("a paralytic," NIV). We don't know exactly what his medical condition was, except that it had so disabled him that he was dependent on others for mobility. He **was borne of** ("carried by," NIV) **four.** When they arrived, others had come earlier and filled up the house and spilled onto the street. The four men saw no way to force their way through the mob while carrying the **bed** ("mat," NIV, NRSV; "pallet," NASB; "stretcher," NEB, HCSB) on which the sick man lay. Luke 5:19 states, "Because of the multitude, they went upon the house top." Houses of that time in Galilee had flat roofs and usually had an outside stairway leading to the roof. William Barclay wrote: "The roof itself was built like this. First, beams were laid from wall to wall, perhaps three feet apart. Timber was usually scarce and the beams had to be sparingly used. Then the spaces between the beams were filled with close-packed reeds and rushes and the branches of thorn bushes. This was filled up and covered over with mortar; and then the whole was topped with a covering of marled earth."[1]

They uncovered the roof where he was literally reads, "they unroofed (*apestegasan*) the roof (*stegen*)." **When they had broken it up** ("after digging through it," NIV), **they let down the bed wherein the sick of the palsy lay.** All of this activity could not have escaped the notice of the people inside the room. We are not told this, but Jesus probably stopped what He was saying and waited for the man to be lowered before Him. We are told that **Jesus saw their faith.** He readily saw what these men had done to get their sick friend to Him.

What were the components of such **faith**? Their actions must have come from a combination of concern and faith. We are not told whether they were relatives, friends, or neighbors; but they must have been concerned enough about the condition of the sick man and they must have cared enough for him to go to all this trouble to bring him to Jesus. They also must have believed that Jesus could heal him. Jesus saw their faith and love in action. He also realized how they had worked together to do what one alone could not have done. He realized that they refused to give up in spite of the obstacles of the crowd and the roof. Thus their faith was in Jesus; was an expression of their love for the needy man; and was cooperative, persistent, and bold. They could have given up when they realized that they could not get through the crowds. Instead, they went on the roof, dug through the roof, and lowered him. This took boldness because of the many risks. Believers today need to have these qualities of love and faith if we are to bring people to Jesus.

Jesus did not view this as an interruption but as an opportunity. Some of His greatest teachings and miracles happened when He was interrupted in something He was doing. His usual practice was to help the person or people who came for help. Those who serve the Lord today must see so-called interruptions as opportunities.

Who was included in the words **when Jesus saw their faith**? Obviously the expression included the four men who carried their friend. Did it also include the sick man? Most Bible students believe that it did. He would not have risked the humiliation without some faith. Also, Jesus forgave his sins. Jesus sometimes healed people without faith, but can you think of anyone whom He forgave without faith? Of course not!

In Jesus' words, **Son, thy sins be forgiven thee,** the term **son** is *teknon*, a warm word for "child" or "son." **Thy sins** makes clear that the paralytic—like everyone else—was a sinner. We are not told whether his sins had led to His sickness, but many Bible students believe that this is inferred from the way the incident is described. If so, true healing had to begin with forgiveness of his sins. Even if his sins had not caused his sickness, Jesus' words show that sin is the basic problem of humanity. True life cannot begin until sins are forgiven by the Lord.

As we saw in the Word Study, **forgiven** is the usual word for forgiveness in the New Testament. The Old Testament gives three powerful analogies of forgiveness. Forgiveness is like having sins as red as blood made as white as snow (Isa. 1:18). Forgiveness is like having our sins removed as far as the east is from the west (Ps. 103:12). Forgiveness is like having our sins thrown into the depths of the sea (Mic. 7:19). The New Testament sees forgiveness as one way to describe salvation. The word is from the areas of human relations and of business. In human relations, forgiveness removes or sets aside the hurt inflicted by someone so that fellowship is restored. In business, it means canceling a debt.

> Forgiven, I've been forgiven;
> God has looked beyond my sin,
> Saved me from what I might have been,
> Gave me a new life within,
> I am forgiven by His grace.[2]

The Religious Leaders' Antagonism (Mark 2:6-7)

Why were the religious leaders so antagonistic toward Jesus? What is blasphemy? Why did they accuse Jesus of this sin? These questions are addressed in comments on these verses.

Verses 6-7: But there were certain of the scribes sitting there, and reasoning in their hearts, ⁷Why doth this man thus speak blasphemies? who can forgive sins but God only?

Scribes were mentioned in Mark 1:22, which quotes the people as comparing the authoritative teaching of Jesus with that of the scribes. Luke 5:21 states that Pharisees were present with the scribes when Jesus forgave the paralytic. Most scribes were Pharisees. The two groups usually appear together. The **scribes** were specialists in interpreting, teaching, and enforcing the Law (both the written Law and their own rules for keeping the Law).

According to verses 6-7, the scribes had not yet put their criticism into words. The scribes were **sitting there, and reasoning in their hearts.** Their opposition would become increasingly more open as time went on. Their thoughts became questions, then accusations, then plots, and finally they condemned Jesus to death. Here they were asking themselves, **Why doth this man thus speak blasphemies? who can forgive sins but God only?** Blasphemy is insulting, defaming, or profaning God. Blasphemy was a serious sin. By forgiving the sick man, Jesus was doing something that only God can do. From the scribes' point of view, Jesus was just another human being— thus He committed this terrible sin by claiming to forgive sin. This was tantamount to claiming to be God! Later, blasphemy would be the sin that the Sanhedrin claimed was grounds for Jesus' being put to death (14:64).

The scribes rightly saw that the words of Jesus, **thy sins be forgiven thee,** were more than a pronouncement that God had forgiven the man's sins. Jesus was claiming authority to forgive sin as the divine Son of man (see vv. 9-10).

If we intend to join Jesus in His search for lost people today, we must be prepared to endure criticism, opposition, and misunderstanding.

Jesus' Authority (Mark 2:8-12)

Why did Jesus heal the man? What was the basis for His claim to the authority to forgive sins? What is the meaning of Jesus as Son of man? What view of Jesus did the crowds have after witnessing this incident? These questions are addressed in comments on these verses.

Verses 8-12: **And immediately when Jesus perceived in his spirit that they so reasoned within themselves, he said unto them, Why reason ye these things in your hearts?** [9]**Whether is it easier to say to the sick of the palsy, Thy sins be forgiven thee; or to say, Arise, and take up thy bed, and walk?** [10]**But that ye may know that the Son of man hath power on earth to forgive sins, (he saith to the sick of the palsy,)** [11]**I say unto thee, Arise, and take up thy bed, and go thy way into thine house.** [12]**And immediately he arose, took up the bed, and went forth before them all; insomuch that they were all amazed, and glorified God, saying, We never saw it on this fashion.**

Jesus perceived in his spirit what they were thinking. He asked them why they had such thoughts. Then He asked, **Whether is it easier to say to the sick of the palsy, Thy sins be forgiven thee; or to say, Arise, and take up thy bed, and walk?** The key words are **easier to say.** How would the scribes have answered that question? Surely they would have said that it is easier to pronounce the forgiveness of sins. No proof would be required; therefore, no one could tell if the words were true. However, to call for a paralytic to walk would require a miracle that could be tested by watching the sick man.

Jesus wanted them to **know that the Son of man hath power on earth to forgive sins.** To show them this, Jesus told the sick man, **Arise, and take up thy bed, and go thy way into thine house.** "He did the miracle which they could see that they might know that he had done the other one which they could not see. Thus there are two miracles here—the physical one and the spiritual. For it is important to note that Jesus claims the power not only to announce the forgiveness of sins, but, as God's representative, actually to forgive them; in short, to come forward as the divine Pardon incarnate."[3]

Someone might say that the words **thy sins be forgiven thee** were not a clear claim to forgive sins. Verse 10 makes clear Jesus' meaning. He claimed **power on earth to forgive sins. Power** is *exousia,* which means "authority" (NIV). Jesus agreed with the scribes that only God can forgive sins, but by forgiving the man He showed that He claimed to be God's Son. The Gospels show that Jesus had authority to forgive sins, and He had authority over sickness. Other incidents show that He also had authority over nature, evil spirits, and even death.

Why did Jesus use the title **Son of man** so often of Himself? There were other titles that people would have recognized as referring to the One whom God would send. "Messiah," "King," and "Son of David" often were used by first-century Jews; **Son of man** was seldom if ever used to refer to the Messiah. Jesus was reluctant to use the more popular messianic titles. He avoided them where possible. He even told people not to tell others that He was the Messiah. He did this because people already had loaded these titles with their own meanings.

Jesus preferred to use a less familiar title and to fill it with His own meaning. As we noted earlier, Jesus used the title Son of man in three different but related ways. He used it of His ministry and His authority. He used it of His coming suffering, death, and resurrection. He used it of His future coming.

Some people misunderstand the meaning of **Son of man.** They assume that it refers to Jesus' humanity and "Son of God" refers to His deity. Actually each title refers to both His full humanity and His full deity. Jesus also used **Son of man** to point to His atoning death for sinners. His role as **Son of man** thus had to do with His authority to forgive sins. When He told the paralytic that his sins were forgiven, He did so based on the love of God revealed at Calvary. Forgiveness is free, but costly. It cost Jesus His life, and it costs the sinner his sins. We can see this dynamic at work in human forgiveness. Suppose someone hurts you. To forgive the person, you must absorb the hurt without striking back. At the cross, Jesus absorbed the hurt of the sins of the world to offer forgiveness to all who repent and believe.

Forgiveness is possible when people repent or turn from their sins (Mark 1:4; Acts 3:19). True repentance always is linked with faith (Mark 1:14-15; Acts 20:21).

The paralyzed man showed his faith by obeying the command of Jesus: **Arise, and take up thy bed, and go thy way into thine house.** The man **immediately** obeyed. This was evidence of his faith in Jesus. It also shows the connection between forgiveness of sins and physical health. If his sickness was caused by his sins, Jesus' forgiveness of his sins set the stage for physical healing. Even if his sickness was not caused by some specific sin, forgiveness made him whole.

A doctor had a patient who was having severe cramps in his abdomen. After a total physical examination, the doctor told the man: "You are all tied up in knots. There is nothing organically wrong with you, yet I believe that you have some deep worry, and I'm afraid that the pain will go on until you get the worry straightened out."

The man replied: "Doctor, about 10 years ago I got tangled up with a woman. It's all over. My wife knows about it, and she's been wonderful. But recently I became an officer in my church, and now this woman threatens to tell my pastor."

The doctor exploded: "Man, go tell him yourself. Sin is his business, the way sickness is mine. It's no surprise to him that people make mistakes and do wrong."

A few weeks later the doctor met the patient, a well man. The removal of the burden of guilt led to release from the physical symptoms he had experienced.[4]

When the paralytic **took up the bed, and went forth before them all,** the people **were all amazed.** They **glorified God, saying, We never saw it on this fashion** ("We have never seen anything like this!" NIV). The Gospels contain many such sayings about the uniqueness of Jesus. They emphasize that Jesus' was more than a man. This unit of study is "No One Else Like Jesus." Anyone reading the Gospels with an open mind and a seeking heart will recognize that Jesus claimed to be unique. The Gospels confront us with a choice. Jesus own term to refer to Himself, **Son of man,** "could refer to an ordinary human being or to a supernatural being. It had overtones of both humanity and deity. By using it, Jesus forced persons to make up their own minds as to what kind of person he was."[5]

Some people try to speak well of Jesus while refusing to accept Him as Son of God and Savior. Many refer to Him as only a great teacher. In his classic work, C. S. Lewis pointed out the fallacy of this: "You must make your choice. Either this man was, and is, the Son of God: or else a madman or something worse."[6]

❖ Spiritual Transformations

The Scripture on which this lesson is based emphasizes the uniqueness of Jesus Christ as the One who can forgive sins. As Christians, we need to commit ourselves to Jesus as Lord and then seek to bring others to Him.

What does it take to bring others to the Lord? It takes faith in the unique Son of man who can save us from sin. It takes concern for others—concern that is strong enough for us to act. It takes perseverance in efforts to bring others to the Lord. It takes boldness that does not fear opposition.

Whom did the Lord use to bring you to Jesus? How did he or she do it? __

_____

Whom do you need to bring to Jesus? How will you seek do it? _____

_____

Prayer of Commitment: Lord, thank You for sending someone to bring me to You; help me to be used by You to bring others to You.

[1]William Barclay, *And He Had Compassion on Them* [Edinburgh: The Church of Scotland Youth Committee, 1959], 51.

[2]Mark Blankenship, "Forgiven," *The Baptist Hymnal* [Nashville: Convention Press, 1991], 341.

[3]A. M. Hunter, *The Gospel According to Saint Mark,* in Torch Bible Commentaries [London: SCM Press, Ltd., 1949), 38.

[4]Andrew W. Blackwood, Jr., *The Voice from the Cross* [Grand Rapids: Baker Book House, 1962], 55.

[5]James A. Brooks, "Mark," in *The New American Commentary,* vol. 23 [Nashville: Broadman Press, 1991], 59.

[6]C. S. Lewis, *Mere Christianity* [New York: The Macmillan Company, 1958], 41.

LOVING MY ENEMIES

Background Passage: Luke 6:12-49
Focal Passage: Luke 6:22,27-38
Key Verse: Luke 6:35

❖ *Significance of the Lesson*

• The *Theme* of this lesson is Jesus expects His followers to love their enemies.

• The *Life Question* this lesson seeks to address is Why should I demonstrate love to my enemies?

• The *Biblical Truth* is that believers demonstrate love to their enemies through deliberate acts of compassion.

• The *Life Impact* is help you act in love toward those who mistreat you.

Christian Love in a Hostile World

Adults struggle with how to live in a hostile world. We have only to listen to the latest news to hear of some of the many forms of hostility. People destroy property, reputations, and lives of others. Most adults have experienced animosity toward them by people who seek to hurt them. The secular world expects people to get even with those who hurt one another.

The biblical worldview taught by Jesus is to love our brothers and sisters in Christ and, indeed, all people—even our enemies. God demonstrated that kind of love by sending Christ to die for people who were His enemies. He expects His children to do the same in showing love to others. Loving enemies is possible with the help of the Spirit of God.

Sermon on the Mount and Sermon on the Plain

This week's lesson is drawn from the Sermon on the Plain in Luke 6. Luke 6:17-49 is called the Sermon on the Plain (based on v. 17). This passage has much in common with Matthew 5–7, which is called the Sermon on the Mount (based on 5:1). These two passages also have some differences. One is much longer than the other, but much of the content in Luke 6:17-49 is also in Matthew 5–7; and most of the rest of Matthew 5–7 is somewhere in Luke. Based on the differences, some Bible students think that these were two sermons delivered on different occasions. Based on the similarities, others think that these passages represent two versions of the same sermon. Still others emphasize that Jesus probably taught the same truths more than once; therefore, both sermons were teachings that He gave on more than one occasion. Jesus gave His Sermon on the Plain near Capernaum during His great Galilean ministry, shortly after He selected His 12 apostles (Mark 3:13-19; Luke 6:12-16).

Both passages present the expectations for followers of Jesus in such a way that these teachings differ radically from the standards of the secular world. Writing about the Sermon on the Mount, John R. W. Stott referred to Jesus' teachings as advocating a "Christian Counter Culture." Usually the expression "counter culture" is used to refer to different secular lifestyles that depart from more traditional cultural values. Stott's point was that Jesus called His followers to live in ways that departed from the common cultural values, except the values He taught represent not just another set of secular values but the values of God's eternal kingdom.[1]

Word Study: *Enemies*

The Greek noun translated enemies in verses 27 and 35 is *echthros*. It comes from the word *echthra*, which means "hostility" and "hatred." When this adjective is used as a noun with something or someone as an object, it too means "enemy." It often is used with the word *miseo*, which means "to hate." Enemies are those who hate others and express that hatred in ways designed to hurt the person who is hated.

Does it sound strange to you that Jesus spoke to His followers about their enemies? Jesus did not entertain the possibility that His disciples had enemies because His disciples took the initiative to reject people. Rather, Jesus referred to believers' enemies as those who take the initiative to demonstrate hostility toward His followers because of their faith in Him.

❖ *Search the Scriptures*

Jesus pronounced His followers blessed when they were hated because of their relation to Him. He warned His followers to expect opposition, act in love rather than react in hatred, return good for evil, and guard their attitudes. He called for His followers to love their enemies. He defined love as acting for the good of the person being loved. Jesus' way stands in striking contrast to the world's way of hating enemies and loving friends.

Expect Opposition (Luke 6:22)

What is the meaning of **blessed**? In what ways do people express their hatred for believers? These questions are addressed in comments on this verse.

Luke 6:22: **Blessed are ye, when men shall hate you, and when they shall separate you from their company, and shall reproach you, and cast out your name as evil, for the Son of man's sake.**

Luke 6:20-26 lists four Beatitudes and four woes. Jesus declared as **blessed** those who are poor, hungry, weeping, and hated for the sake of the Son of man. Then He gave four woes on those who are rich, well-fed, happy, and popular. The fourth of the blessings is in verse 22.

The word **blessed** introduces each Beatitude. Translators struggle with how to translate the Greek word *makarioi*. Some have used the word "happy" and explained the Beatitudes as the divine formula for human happiness. The contents and structure of Luke 6:17-49, however, describe God's blessing on those who belong to His eternal kingdom. These words are not a prescription for human happiness. The central issue is how God evaluates us, not how happy we feel. Being **blessed** in this context means that our actions meet with God's approval.

Luke 6:22-23 is similar in meaning to the Beatitude in Matthew 5:10-12, although most of the wording is different. Matthew 5:10-11 pronounces a blessing on those "which are persecuted for righteousness' sake," and Luke used **when men shall hate you.** The kind of hatred Jesus had in mind—in Luke as well as in Matthew—came from hatred that grows out of persecution. It was **for the Son of man's sake.**

Hate is *miseo.* Three other negative actions toward believers are listed in verse 22. These are expressions of hatred. First, **they shall separate you from their company.** The word for **separate you,** *aphopisosin,* can mean "exclude" (NIV, HCSB). Some Bible students think that this meant exclusion from the synagogue, which sometimes happened (see John 9:22,34). However, it more likely refers to any exclusion of followers of Christ from some group—family, business, community, and so forth.

The second negative action against believers is that they **shall reproach you. Reproach** translates *oneidisosin,* which means to "revile" (NRSV) or "insult" (NIV, HCSB, NASB). It refers to the slander to which believers are subjected. The early believers often were misunderstood and slandered.

Much of this came from the people in general who did not understand the Christians. Believers were accused of all kinds of sins: atheism (not believing in the pagan gods), cannibalism (from hearing the words of the Lord's Supper), immorality (from the love feasts). The Roman historian Tacitus vividly described the persecution of Christians by Nero. The rumor had spread that Nero himself was responsible for the great fire that destroyed much of Rome. Tacitus wrote, "To get rid of this rumor, Nero set up as the culprits and punished with the utmost refinement of cruelty a class hated for their abominations, which are commonly called Christians. Christus, from whom their name is derived, was executed at the hands of the procurator Pontius Pilate in the reign of Tiberius. Checked for the moment, this pernicious superstition again broke out, not only in Judaea, the source of the evil, but even in Rome, that receptacle of everything that is sordid and degrading."[2]

The third negative action against believers is that they would **cast out your name as evil.** This is a literal translation of the Greek. **Cast out** is *ekbalosin*, which literally is to "throw out." The Greeks sometimes used it of hissing an actor off the stage. A person's **name** stood for the person's character and reputation. This statement reinforces the two previous ones. Those who serve Jesus faithfully will find that when Jesus Himself is rejected, so shall they be.

Luke 6:1-11, especially verse 11, shows how such opposition to Jesus was already becoming nasty. If the disciples truly represented the **Son of man,** they must be ready to follow Him in the way of the cross (9:23).

The direct application of these verses is to situations involving persecution. Persecution is a reality in many areas of today's world. People are deprived of their possessions, their jobs, their reputations, and even their lives simply because they are Christians. But these verses apply to anyone seeking to follow Jesus by doing right. They do not apply when people hate us for doing wrong. Sometime later, Peter similarly urged Christians to be sure they suffered only because of doing good, not for doing evil (1 Pet. 4:15-16). The point is that anyone who is committed to Jesus Christ should expect to experience opposition and rejection from some people, but such believers are nevertheless blessed by God and under His approval.

Act Rather Than React (Luke 6:27-31)

Who are our enemies? How can Christians love their enemies? How literally are the illustrations in verses 29-30 to be taken? How can Christians practice the Golden Rule? These questions are addressed in comments on these verses.

Verse 27-28: **But I say unto you which hear, Love your enemies, do good to them which hate you. **[28]**Bless them that curse you, and pray for them which despitefully use you.**

Jesus spoke to those **which hear.** This means that they heed what they hear. The final verses of the Sermon on the Plain stress this (vv. 46-49).

This and other focal verses in this lesson describe how to live in light of verse 22. **Love your enemies** is probably the most difficult of all Jesus' teachings—both to understand and to practice. **Enemies** are those who show they are enemies by doing the four things in verse 22. Two others are added in verses 27-28—**curse you** and **despitefully use you.** Because we are follow-ers of Christ, believers are to **love** those who do these things to us. Although the primary application is to persecution, the command to love enemies applies to anyone who hates us. **Love** is *agapao.* This is the verb form of *agape.* The tense of this and the other three verbs in verses 27-28 call for continuous action. We are to keep on loving our enemies.

How can anyone **love** an enemy? Enemies are by definition people who oppose and hurt us because they hate us. The key is in the meaning of *aga-pao,* which is described in three ways in verses 27-28, illustrated in four ways in verses 29-30, and summed up in verse 31. *Agapao* refers not to emotions so much as to actions. Loving our enemies does not mean having a warm, fuzzy feeling about them. Basically, it means to **do good to them which hate you.** You don't have to feel affection for an enemy before you love him. If that were true, we seldom would be able to achieve this radical kind of love. It means to do good for our enemies, no matter how we feel about them.

This insight first came to me when I read *Mere Christianity* by C. S. Lewis. He wrote, "A good many people imagine that forgiving your enemies means making out that they are really not such bad fellows after all, when it is quite plain that they are."[3] Robert H. Stein, writing in the *New American Commen-tary,* commented, "The command to love one's enemies is not directed to how believers are to feel but how they are to act. Often loving feelings follow loving actions much like a caboose follows an engine. Jesus' commands, how-ever, are addressed to the engine of the will and not the caboose of feelings."[4]

Bless them that curse you is another means of showing love for enemies. This command moves from actions that are good to our words. Enemies do **curse** Christians. The natural human response is to call down judgment on them. Instead, we are to **bless them.** Blessing someone means to ask God's favor on that person. We can do some good for our enemies, but God can do much more. The command differs from the usual practice of blessing friends and cursing enemies.

Pray for them which despitefully use ("mistreat," NIV, HCSB, NASB; "abuse," NRSV) **you** is the third means of showing love for enemies. The verb for treating someone with malice and spite appears in the New Testament only here and in 1 Peter 3:16. Christians are to **pray** for such people, in spite of the mistreatment suffered at their hands.

Jesus' command for His follows to love their enemies is not the first time someone said such a thing; however, Jesus was the first to practice it perfectly and to empower His followers to do the same. As Jesus died on the cross, He prayed for the forgiveness of His tormentors (Luke 23:34). Stephen made a similar prayer when he was dying (Acts 7:58-60). Paul and Peter taught the same thing (Rom. 12:16-21; 1 Pet. 3:9).

Verses 29-30: **And unto him that smiteth thee on the one cheek offer also the other; and him that taketh away thy cloak forbid not to take thy coat also.** ³⁰**Give to every man that asketh of thee; and of him that taketh away thy goods ask them not again.**

Jesus then gave four illustrations of how to practice love for enemies. Bible students have struggled to understand and to do what Jesus taught in these verses. They have wondered if these words were meant to be rules that are to be followed literally or illustrations of principles by which to live. Many have concluded that these four illustrations were not intended to become absolute commands so much as exaggerations designed to reinforce the teaching to love our enemies. Many of us believe that these examples apply to us on a personal level; they do not apply to governments, which are ordained by God to protect societies against criminals. Neither are they designed to call for us to stand idly by when innocents are mistreated by wicked people.

The first illustration calls for offering the other **cheek** to those who strike you on one **cheek. Smiteth** is *tuptonti*, which means "hits" (HCSB, REB) or "strikes" (NIV, NKJV). **Cheek** is *siagona*, which some commentators translate as "jaw." Thus Jesus could have been referring to a punch in the jaw or to a slap on the cheek. More likely He meant the backhanded slap, which was an insult.

Jesus was showing His followers how to respond to this or to any other insult directed against one personally. When we are injured or insulted—whether by words or by a blow—our inclination is to retaliate. Jesus taught us instead to absorb the insult without striking back, even if this means making ourselves vulnerable to further abuses.

The second illustration deals with clothing. **Taketh away** seems to refer to robbery. **Cloak** referred to one's outer garment. **Coat** ("tunic," NIV; "shirt," NASB, NRSV, HCSB) was an inner garment. In contemporary English we would say, "If someone steals your coat, don't withhold your shirt also." We speak of "giving the shirt off our back," but we usually are thinking of friends who need what we can give to them. Jesus, however, was speaking of an enemy. The point of this exaggerated example is to contrast it with the normal human reaction to regain what is ours. Again, this does not mean that the government is not to punish thieves and robbers.

The third illustration is to **give to every man that asketh of thee.** This applies not only to family and friends who ask for help but also to strangers, even to enemies. The setting applies to borrowing and to begging.

The fourth illustration again refers to one who **taketh away**; this time to **him that taketh away thy goods. Taketh away** is *airontos,* the same word as in verse 29. This applies to any taking of our property. It includes robbery, confiscation, or looting. Hebrews 10:32-34 describes a time when believers "were publicly exposed to insult and persecution" and "accepted the confiscation of [their] property." They were able to do this because they knew that they "had better and lasting possessions" (NIV). Thus Jesus said to **ask them not again** or "do not demand it back" (NIV) when someone takes away something that is yours. These last three of the four examples apply to loss of property. Jesus used these three extreme examples to show that we should be compassionate, forbearing, and generous. Examples 2 and 4 apply when our possessions are taken away. The second applies when someone asks us to give or lend them something that is ours. All of these go counter to the normal way of claiming our rights to what is ours.

Keep in mind that these are exaggerations of basic principles that are contrary to the way people normally react with demands for restitution or in retaliation. Of course, if we literally gave to everyone who asked for us to give to them, we could be unable to care for our own families. Each of us have limited resources in a world of unlimited needs. We must be faithful stewards of the resources God has given to us and we must follow His leadership in setting priorities for giving. This should be done generously and sacrificially.

Verse 31: **And as ye would that men should do to you, do ye also to them likewise.**

This is the Golden Rule. Others before Jesus had stated something like this. Many moralists have stated a negative form of the rule. For example, Confucius, in the *Analects* (15.23), said, "What you do not want done to yourself, do not do to others." The uniqueness of Jesus' Golden Rule is that it is stated positively and emphatically. He taught us to think how we would want to be treated if we were in the place of the other person. Then we are to take the initiative in treating the person that way. The exercise of Christian love is not dependent on other' behavior.

Return Good for Evil (Luke 6:32-36)

How do Jesus' teachings differ from the usual ways that non-Christians act? What is the motivation and power to live by Jesus' teachings? These questions are addressed in comments on these verses.

Verses 32-34: **For if ye love them which love you, what thank have ye? for sinners also love those that love them. [33]And if ye do good to them which do good to you, what thank have ye? for sinners also do even the same. [34]And if ye lend to them of whom ye hope to receive, what thank have ye? for sinners also lend to sinners, to receive as much again.**

These verses give three examples drawn from verses 27 and 30: love for enemies, doing good for them, and giving freely to them. Verses 32-34 show the usual ways of acting in each case. Two words need clarification: **thank** and **sinners. Thank** is *charis*, which here has the idea of "credit." "If you love those who love you, what credit is that to you?" (NIV). "If you love only someone who loves you, will God praise you for that?" (CEV).

Sinners is an accurate translation, but what does it mean here? Jesus intended to refer to the natural way of life among those who do not know Him. Jesus taught His followers to love all people, not just family and friends. Loving those who love us is normal and natural for human beings. The same is true of doing **good** for others. Jesus called His followers to **do good** for enemies; the normal way is to **do good to them which do good for you.** The same contrast is seen in lending and borrowing. If you **lend to them of whom ye hope to receive,** you're no different from anyone else. Even non-Christians do that.

These are three examples of how Jesus' expectations of His followers represent a counter culture to secular society. Even **sinners** love those who love them, do good to those who do good to them, and lend to those from whom they expect to receive back what they loan. Only those empowered by the Spirit of the Lord are motivated and empowered to love enemies, do good for them, and freely lend to anyone who asks.

Verses 35-36: **But love ye your enemies, and do good, and lend, hoping for nothing again; and your reward shall be great, and ye shall be the children of the Highest: for he is kind unto the unthankful and to the evil. [36]Be ye therefore merciful, as your Father also is merciful.**

In contrast to the usual ways of acting, Christians are to **love their enemies, and do good, and lend, hoping for nothing again. Hoping** includes desiring and expecting. In **your reward shall be great,** what is the **reward**? Is it not to be seen as **children of the Highest**? This is God's way of dealing with sinners. He loved us while we were yet sinners (Rom. 5:6-8). **He is kind unto the unthankful and to the evil.**

We are to love enemies, do good for them, and freely give to them because this is how God has dealt with us. **Be ye therefore merciful, as your Father also is merciful.** God in Christ has shown mercy and self-giving love to us while we were enemies to Him. Now He calls us to allow Him to work in and through us to do the same toward others who are enemies to Him and to us as His followers. This is the motivation and the source of power for us to live by these demands. We have not only His example, but we also have His Spirit within us to empower us to love as He loves.

Guard Your Attitude (Luke 6:37-38)

Why are Christians not to judge or condemn others? How is God's forgiveness of our sins related to our forgiveness of those who sin against us? How does the measure of our giving relate to that which we receive from God? These questions are addressed in comments on these verses.

Verses 37-38: **Judge not, and ye shall not be judged: condemn not, and ye shall not be condemned: forgive, and ye shall be forgiven: [38]give, and it shall be given unto you; good measure, pressed down, and shaken together, and running over, shall men give into your bosom. For with the same measure that ye mete withal it shall be measured to you again.**

Jesus taught His followers to **judge not** and to **condemn not.** Judging as used here is not of judgments rendered by governments. Neither is it the same as making evaluations of others. In verses 43-45, Jesus said that we should apply the test of fruitfulness in evaluating ourselves and others. In verses 37-38, Jesus was warning against prejudice, hasty judgment, and critical judgment. **Judge** and **condemn** are parallel. To judge someone is to condemn the person. Only God is qualified to judge and condemn. Only He has all the facts, and only He has the character of the Ultimate Judge; only He is perfectly just and merciful.

Jesus warned that judgmental people will be judged and that people who condemn others will themselves be condemned. In verses 41-42, He challenged judgmental people to look at their own lives with the same scrutiny that they apply to others.

Over against a judgmental spirit Jesus set two positive things to do: **forgive** and **give.** Forgiveness is essential in loving anyone—Christians and enemies. Jesus thus linked together forgiving others with receiving God's forgiveness. Forgiveness is a two-way street. The person whose heart is open for divine forgiveness is open also for forgiveness to flow out to others. The person whose heart is closed to forgiving others is closed also to receiving God's forgiveness.

By the same token, **give, and it shall be given unto you.** Christians should **give** generously. If someone was giving grain, the container should be **pressed down, and shaken together, and running over.** Instead of trying to make the amount look larger than it is, Jesus told them to press down the grain in its container, shake it so that every space will be filled, and then fill it to running over.

The general rule of thumb for all these things is that we determine the standards by which God and others judge, condemn, forgive, and give to us. The generous person will receive generously from the Lord. Our giving basket is the size of our receiving basket.

Ernest Gordon spent over three years in Japanese POW camps during World War II. His book *Through the Valley of the Kwai* is an amazing account of Christian love in action—under the worst of conditions. The Japanese were determined to break the spirit of their prisoners, and for a time they succeeded. The prisoners lived by the law of the jungle. They fought over scraps of food; they stole from one another; they ignored the weak, the sick, the dying. Then the actions of a few began to change the whole camp. These few believers began to practice the teachings of Jesus.

They began by reaching out to help one another. They helped the weak, cared for the sick, comforted the dying, and reverently buried the dead. Their loving spirit spread. Other prisoners began to study the New Testament, especially the Sermon on the Mount. Yet when they said the Model Prayer, they stumbled through the part about forgiving others. Their guards had treated them so brutally that the prisoners hated the Japanese and hoped for some way to get even.

Some, however, began to do good even for their despised guards. For example, a train loaded with wounded Japanese soldiers stopped nearby. The Christian prisoners gave food and water to these pitiful soldiers, who were being ignored even by their own countrymen. Gordon wrote, "Eighteen months ago they would have joined readily in the destruction of our captors. . . . Now these same officers were dressing the enemy's wounds."[5] When the war was over, the Allied soldiers who liberated them wanted to kill the guards for what they had done to the prisoners. Only the intervention of the Christian prisoners stopped this vengeful fury.

❖ *Spiritual Transformations*

Jesus said that believers are blessed when they are hated because of their relation with Him. He called for Christians to love their enemies by doing good for them. He contrasted this kind of love with that of sinners who love only those who love them. Jesus warned against condemning others and called for generous forgiving and giving.

One of the greatest spiritual transformations is to move from loving only ourselves and those who love us to loving God and loving others, even our enemies. Sinful people love one another. Only Christ's power can motivate and empower people to love their enemies. This love calls for a commitment of will because such love is doing good for others, not feeling deep affection for them.

Do you find it easy to love people who love you? to do good to people who do good by you? _____

_____

How do you feel about people who hurt you? about those who use you? ___

_____

What has been your experience in loving people who hurt you? _____

_____

How strong is your commitment to do good for others, even enemies? _____

_____

Prayer of Commitment: Lord, help me to be motivated and empowered to love even those who hurt me.

[1]John R. W. Stott, *The Message of the Sermon on the Mount,* in The Bible Speaks Today Series [Downers Grove: InterVarsity Press, 1978], 15-16.

[2]Tacitus, *Annales,* xv. 44, in *Documents of the Christian Church,* edited by Henry Bettenson [New York: Oxford University Press, 1947], 4.

[3]C. S. Lewis, *Mere Christianity* [New York: The Macmillan Company, 1958], 90.

[4]Robert H. Stein, "Luke," in *The New American Commentary,* vol. 24 [Nashville: Broadman Press, 1992], 206-207.

[5]Ernest Gordon, *Through the Valley of the Kwai* [New York: Harper & Brothers, Publishers, 1962], 222.

KNOWING JESUS CARES

Background Passage: Mark 4:35–5:20
Focal Passage: Mark 4:35-39; 5:6-9,15-20
Key Verse: Mark 5:19

❖ *Significance of the Lesson*

• The *Theme* of this lesson is Jesus cares about people in need.
• The *Life Question* this lesson seeks to address is How can I know that Jesus cares about me?
• The *Biblical Truth* is that believers can have the assurance of Jesus' concern for them as they experience His healing presence in the storms and turmoil of life.
• The *Life Impact* is to help you depend on the compassionate Christ.

Does Jesus Care?

Many adults struggle with feelings of loneliness and alienation. They feel separated from the people around them. Many also doubt the existence of a personal God who is concerned about them and their needs. They may believe that if God exists at all, He is remote from them, unconcerned with and uninvolved in their personal problems.

The biblical worldview is built on the foundation of a personal God who cares about people. This God revealed that concern in Jesus. People of faith see the love of God revealed in Jesus, and they experience His love in the midst of life's difficulties. God does not always deliver them from troubles, but He is always with them in those times.

Demon Possession and Exorcisms

The Scriptures carefully distinguish between demon possession and various illnesses (see Matt. 4:23-24). The Gospels tell of some specific exorcisms. The first miracle recorded in Mark's Gospel was casting out an unclean spirit from a man in the synagogue in Capernaum (Mark 1:23-27). In addition to specific miracles, casting out demons is included in the general lists of miracles (vv. 32-34). Those persons who were possessed by demons demonstrated features incompatible with a view that they were merely physically or mentally ill. Jesus dealt with cases of demon possession as realities. The healing of the man in Mark 5:1-20 reveals symptoms that would not be produced by epilepsy or insanity. Jesus said that His casting out demons showed that the kingdom of God had come near (Luke 11:20).

Demoniacs were sometimes portrayed as victims and sometimes as morally responsible for their plight (Luke 11:24-26). In either case, the person possessed by demons was unable to deliver himself from the plight. In this sense, the demon-possessed are like many people today whose lives are out of control. They are enslaved to powers and forces from which they cannot set themselves free.

Word Study: *Legion*

Legion is the name of a unit in the Roman army. In the time of Augustus it consisted of about 6,000 men with about the same number of auxiliaries. Jesus used the word in Matthew 26:53 when He said that He could call 12 legions of angels to His aid if He chose to do so. In Mark 5:9 the demoniac gave "Legion" as his name. It probably means that he was possessed by "lots" (CEV) of demons.

❖ *Search the Scriptures*

When Jesus slept during a dangerous storm, the disciples asked Him if He really cared about them. The demoniac cried out who Jesus was and gave his own name as "Legion." After Jesus cast the demons out of him, the man was totally changed; but the people asked Jesus to leave their area. The man wanted to go with Jesus, but the Lord told him to return to his home and tell others how God had shown compassion on him. These two events in the life and ministry of Jesus demonstrate that Jesus cares and has compassion on those in need—an announcement we need to share with others.

A Storm Stilled (Mark 4:35-39)

What did the disciples ask Jesus when a storm threatened them? How did Jesus respond to their words? These questions are addressed in comments on these verses.

Mark 4:35-39: **And the same day, when the even was come, he saith unto them, Let us pass over unto the other side. ³⁶And when they had sent away** the multitude, they took him even as he was in the ship. And there were also with him other little ships. [37]And there arose a great storm of wind, and the waves beat into the ship, so that it was now full. [38]And he was in the hinder part of the ship, asleep on a pillow: and they awake him, and say unto him, Master, carest thou not that we perish? [39]And he arose, and rebuked the wind, and said unto the sea, Peace, be still. And the wind ceased, and there was a great calm.

Jesus had been teaching the multitudes earlier in the day by the seaside (Mark 4:1-2). **And the same day, when the even** ("evening," NIV) **was come,** Jesus told the disciples to cross the Sea of Galilee to **the other side.** That is, they left the western shore and headed for the eastern shore. After sending **away the multitude,** they began the boat trip. The words **even as he was** probably mean that they did not stop to get provisions. Jesus had been teaching from the boat (v. 1); therefore, they may have left without going ashore.

The Sea of Galilee is below sea level and is surrounded by mountains. This combination makes it subject to sudden storms as warm air clashes with cooler air. On this trip, the disciples experienced **a great storm of wind** ("a furious squall," NIV). The seriousness of the storm is seen in the vivid description of it. **Waves beat into the ship** ("waves broke over the boat," NIV). The *King James Version* describes the ship as **full** of water. Other translations assume that *gemizesthai* means that it was becoming full—"it was nearly swamped" (NIV).

Where was Jesus during this life-threatening storm? He was **in the hinder part** ("stern," NIV, HCSB) **of the ship, asleep on a pillow.** Jesus had put in an exhausting day, and He was worn out. This is the only biblical record of Jesus' sleeping. This testifies to the reality of His humanity as well as to His trust in the Heavenly Father.

To the terrified disciples, Jesus' sleeping seemed to be evidence of His unconcern for them in their plight. Thus **they awake him, and say unto him, Master, carest thou not that we perish?** or "Teacher, don't you care if we drown?" (NIV). **Carest** is *melei,* which means "to care" or "to be concerned." *Melei* often was used by people asking the Lord to show mercy on them in their problems and illnesses.

Jesus **rebuked the wind, and said unto the sea, Peace, be still.** "'Peace' renders a word which means to be silent, still, or calm. 'Be still' means literally, 'Be muzzled.'"[1] The *New International Version* reads, "Quiet! Be still!" The *Holman Christian Standard Bible* has "Silence! Be still!" **Rebuked** (*epetimesen*) and **be still** (*pephimoso*) also are used in the first miracle in Mark—the casting out of a demon in the synagogue at Capernaum (1:25). At this, **the wind ceased, and there was a great calm.**

Jesus asked His disciples about their fear and their lack of faith. They in turn asked, "Who is this? Even the wind and the waves obey him!" (NIV).

The passage illustrates one of the nature miracles of Jesus in which He showed His power and His compassion. The disciples were so awed that they wondered at One who could stop a storm with a command. They had doubted His care for them during the storm, but they had called on Him for help—and He came to their rescue.

The disciples' question in verse 38 is asked by many people in every generation. Everyone experiences storms—literal ones and figurative ones. Jonah and Paul experienced literal storms at sea. Psalm 42:7 describes life's troubles in terms of a storm. When storms come, people often wonder why a good God allows storms. Many people pray for deliverance from both literal and figurative storms. When the storms continue, some people ask the disciples' question, "Don't You care?" When storms of life sweep down on us, Jesus sometimes seems to be asleep—either unaware of or unconcerned for us in our plight. Sometimes when we pray, He stills the storm; but sometimes the storm continues to rage—and our question becomes even more insistent: "Lord, do You really care? If so, why did You allow this to happen to me? And why do You not answer my prayer and deliver me from this?" Faith is belief that the Lord can still the storms of life and trust that if He does not do so He will bring some good out of the evil situation.

We Christians believe that the God of the universe revealed Himself in Jesus Christ. Therefore, we see God's care about people in the care and concern of Jesus His Son. Many people deny that God knows or cares. They base their skepticism on the evil and troubles of life on earth and on the failure of God to answer their prayers for deliverance from the storms of life. Believers live in the same world and see the same storms, yet because of Jesus' care, we believe that God knows and cares. He does not always deliver us from our plight, but He is always with us and He brings us through into His eternal kingdom.

> Jesu, Deliverer!
>   Come Thou to me:
> Soothe Thou my voyaging
>   Over Life's sea!
> Thou, when the storm of Death
>   Roars, sweeping by,
> Whisper, O Truth of Truth!
>   —'Peace! It is I!'[2]

A Need Identified (Mark 5:6-9)

What was the plight of the man in these verses? How did he react toward Jesus? How did Jesus respond to the man's words and actions? What is the significance of the man's name? These questions are addressed in comments on these verses.

Mark 5:6-9: **But when he saw Jesus afar off, he ran and worshiped him, [7]and cried with a loud voice, and said, What have I to do with thee, Jesus, thou Son of the most high God? I adjure thee by God, that thou torment me not. [8]For he said unto him, Come out of the man, thou unclean spirit. [9]And he asked him, What is thy name? And he answered, saying, My name is Legion: for we are many.**

Verses 1-5 provide the setting and describe this poor man's plight. Since Jesus' voyage across the lake began at evening, it was probably night when the disciples and Jesus arrived on the eastern shore of the Sea of Galilee. They were in Gentile territory in "the country of the Gadarenes" (5:1; "Gerasenes," NIV, HCSB). A man with an unclean spirit met them. People had unsuccessfully tried to keep him chained, but he broke the chains. Now he was living among the tombs and cutting himself with rocks. He was the epitome of a hopeless, helpless man.

Put yourself in the place of the disciples. You have just survived a storm at sea. Now in the dark, on an unknown shore, a wild man comes running at you. **Worshiped** is one meaning of *prosekunesen,* but here it probably means "fell on his knees in front of him" (NIV). The man was shouting, **What have I to do with thee, Jesus, thou Son of the most high God?** Demon-possessed people seem to have recognized Jesus and feared Him. Mark 1:24 records an earlier confrontation with such a person, who said: "Let us alone; what have we to do with thee, thou Jesus of Nazareth? art thou come to destroy us? I know thee who thou art, the Holy One of God." The man in 1:24 had some of the same characteristics as the man in 5:1-20: (1) He knew who Jesus was. (2) He asked Jesus not to harm him or them. (3) He referred to himself as both singular and plural.

Torment me not probably refers to the place of punishment awaiting the devil and his demons. Notice he used **me;** but he gave his name as **Legion,** which implies many demons possessed him—or as he put it, **for we are many.** An army of demons possessed this pitiful man. It is hard to tell when the man was speaking for himself and when the demons were speaking through him. Perhaps that explains the man's ambivalence about Jesus. On the one hand, he had run up to Jesus as if seeking His help. Yet at the same time, he was backing away and asking Jesus to let him alone. Many people who need Jesus and are not demon possessed do these same things. On the one hand, they are drawn to Jesus; on the other hand, they fear that He will destroy their old way of life.

The man is identified as "a man with an unclean spirit" (v. 2). In verse 8 Jesus said, **Come out of the man, thou unclean spirit. Unclean spirit** ("Evil spirit," NIV; *to pneuma to akatharton*) is synonymous with the word for "demon" (*daimonion*). *Daimonion* does not appear in Mark 5:1-20, but the verb *daimonizomai* ("to be possessed by a demon") appears in verses 16 and 18. The *King James Version* translates *daimonion* as "devil"; however, the word is "demon." Satan is sometimes called "the prince of demons" (Mark 3:22, NIV).

All the time **Jesus** had been saying, **Come out of the man, thou unclean spirit.** Hobbs noted that the tense of **he said,** *elegen,* is imperfect. Thus it refers to repeated action. Jesus "had repeatedly been saying, Come out of the man, thou unclean spirit."[3]

Verses 3-9 reveal the man's pitiful condition. He was in what seemed to be a hopeless and helpless plight. Other people had tried to help him or at least to restrain him. He is probably the worst case of demon possession recorded in the Gospels. At least the description of his plight is the longest. He is in many ways like people in every generation who are under the control of evil forces—whether demons or evil addictions of various kinds. They are enslaved or possessed by powers stronger than they are.

Some people whose lives are out of control are not so dangerous or violent as this man, but many have these things in common: (1) They have some condition over which they have little or no control. (2) As a result, they are excluded from normal social life and contacts. (3) People who try to help them often are frustrated in their efforts and often give up in despair. (4) Jesus has both the compassion and the power to help such people.

Verses 10-14 describe what happened. The demons asked permission to enter into some swine that were nearby. Jesus gave them permission. The demons entered the swine, and the swine ran to their death over a cliff. Many explanations have been offered for why Jesus allowed this to happen. But perhaps Walter W. Wessel was correct when he suggested that the destruction of the swine in some way was related to the man's cure. Wessel wrote, "A tentative answer is that Jesus wanted to give tangible evidence to the man and to the people that the demons actually had left him and that their purpose had been to destroy him even as they destroyed the pigs."[4]

Mark 5:1-20 is part of the Gospel of Mark that shows Jesus as Lord with authority over all things. This includes nature (4:35-41), demons (5:1-20), disease (vv. 25-34), and death (vv. 22-24,35-43). All of Jesus' actions related to these were acts of compassion, which clearly show the power and love of Jesus as Son of God. They show that Jesus' compassion extends to physical, mental, and spiritual needs.

A Miracle Witnessed (Mark 5:15-17)

How was the man changed? Why did the people ask Jesus to leave? These questions are addressed in comments on these verses.

Mark 5:15-17: **And they come to Jesus, and see him that was possessed with the devil, and had the legion, sitting, and clothed, and in his right mind: and they were afraid. [16]And they that saw it told them how it befell to him that was possessed with the devil, and also concerning the swine. [17]And they began to pray him to depart out of their coasts.**

The tenders of the pigs had witnessed what happened. They spread the news, and people gathered to see for themselves. They found the pigs gone and **him that was possessed with the devil** ("the demoniac,"NRSV; from *daimoni-zomenon*, which is related to the noun *daimonion* or "demon") ... **sitting,** instead of screaming and cutting himself with stones in the tombs. He was **clothed,** instead of being naked. He was **in his right mind,** rather then being controlled by evil spirits. A remarkable transformation obviously had taken place. Jesus had done what none of them or the man himself had been able to do.

Nothing is such a testimony to the compassion of Jesus as a life that is saved and transformed. When Jesus delivers someone from a life of slavery to sin and transforms that life to one that glorifies God, He shows the compassion and power of God. People who doubt the power or concern of God need to look at such people and turn to the Lord themselves.

We might expect the people to praise God and to thank Jesus for this miracle. Instead, **they were afraid.** Their fear was not the reverent awe from seeing the results of a miracle from God. **They began to pray** ("to plead with," NIV) **him to depart out of their coasts.** The key words in verse 16 may be **concerning the swine.** Most Bible students see their request that Jesus leave based on their fear that He would bring ruin to other possessions of theirs. If so, their concern was more with possessions than people. They put financial profits before the welfare of a needy human being. When Paul and his helpers were in Philippi, Paul delivered a young woman from the power of evil spirits. Her owners were upset because they had been using the slave girl as a source of profit. "When her masters saw that the hope of their gains was gone, they caught Paul and Silas, and drew them into the marketplace unto the rulers" (Acts 16:19).

Thus we have in verse 15 a dramatic example of how God can transform and redeem a life out of control. And we have in verses 16-17 an example of the way the world responds to this miracle of grace. Believers should join the heavenly hosts in praising God when even one sinner is saved. But rather than rejoicing, many either are opposed or indifferent. Even some church members seem unmoved when someone is saved. Instead, we should share in heaven's joy over one sinner who repents (Luke 15:7,10).

An Obedient Response (Mark 5:18-20)

What request did the man make of Jesus? What did Jesus tell the man to do? What did the man do? These questions are addressed in comments on these verses.

Mark 5:18-20: And when he was come into the ship, he that had been possessed with the devil prayed him that he might be with him. [19]Howbeit Jesus suffered him not, but saith unto him, Go home to thy friends, and tell them how great things the Lord hath done for thee, and hath had compassion on thee. [20]And he departed, and began to publish in Decapolis how great things Jesus had done for him: and all men did marvel.

Jesus got **into the ship** as He prepared to go back to the western side of the lake. Then **he that had been possessed with the devil** ("demon-possessed," NIV; *daimonistheis*) **prayed** ("begged," NIV) **him that he might be with him.** It is not surprising that the man wanted to go with Jesus. He wanted to be near Him, learn from Him, and serve Him. This ought to be the desire of every person whom Jesus has saved from sin and death.

Howbeit Jesus suffered him not. Suffered does not mean to endure pain. In the English of 1611 it meant "to allow something" or "to give permission." Jesus did not refuse to allow the man to go with Him because the man would not have made a good disciple. He did it because He had something for him to do that only he could do. Jesus told the transformed man, **Go home to thy friends. Friends** is sometimes translated "family" (NIV). *Sous* means "yours," and can refer to family or friends. Jesus literally said, "Go to the ones who are yours." Since a circle wider than just his relatives probably is meant, those translations that have "Go to your people" are helpful (see the NASB, HCSB, REB). Verse 20 shows that he went all over the region. One's family is the place to start. Friends should be included, but sharing the good news of what Jesus has done should not be limited only to family and friends. Jesus' words show His care and concern also extended to the man's family—and beyond.

He told his testimony **in Decapolis.** This was a confederation of 10 Greek cities, which had been founded following the victories of Alexander the

Great. It was a Gentile area. "Mark probably saw in the man the first missionary to the Gentiles and a preview of the Gentile mission that flourished during the quarter century before the writing of his Gospel."[5]

In verse 19 Jesus told the man, **Tell them how great things the Lord hath done for thee. The Lord** may refer to Jesus or to God. As the Son of God, Jesus' work was the work of His Father. In verse 20 the man told **how great things Jesus had done for him.** By telling what Jesus had done for him, he was testifying to what God had done for him. Christians believe that God has revealed Himself most fully in His Son, Jesus Christ. Therefore, in the words and actions of Jesus, we see God the Father. The compassionate Christ means a compassionate God.

Hath had compassion is *eleesen,* which means "to show mercy." The frightened disciples had asked the Lord if He really cared for them (4:38). Jesus' actions showed that He did. Mark 5:19 shows that the Lord also cared for the demoniac. He showed him mercy and compassion by delivering him from the evil spirits that had possessed him.

Why did Jesus encourage this man to tell what had happened when He had told people in Jewish territory not to tell what He had done for them? (1:42-44). The difference is that the healed demoniac of 5:1-20 was to witness in Gentile territory. The ones forbidden to tell were in Jewish areas. The Jews had false ideas about the Messiah; therefore, Jesus wanted to avoid people hearing of His miracles and thinking that He was their false kind of Messiah.

The man obeyed. He **began to publish in Decapolis how great things Jesus had done for him.** No doubt his family and friends were amazed. They knew what kind of person he had been when he was under the power of the demons. His family and friends probably had been the main ones who tried to help him be delivered, but they had been unsuccessful in their efforts. What a joy it must have been when he returned home a new man! When they asked what had changed him, he gladly told them how the Lord had shown mercy on him and transformed him.

The place to begin in giving our testimony for Christ ought to be our family and friends. Andrew went first to his brother Simon (John 1:40-42). Philip went to his friend Nathanael (vv. 45-46). Levi (Matthew) invited his friends and associates to a dinner so he could introduce them to Jesus (Luke 5:29).

Roger and Vicki Grossman, International Mission Board missionaries to Guatemala, told of a man who had an experience like that of the man in this week's lesson. The man's name was Rudy, and he had been drunk and living on the streets for months. One night he came into a worship service led by mission volunteers from the United States. When he bowed his head and asked the Lord to enter his life, some who knew him wondered if he would even remember that night when he sobered up the next morning. Earlier in the same day, Douglas, a cocaine user, also had been saved.

Over the next few months, Rudy and Douglas led over 70 of their family members, friends, and neighbors to the Lord while maintaining their testimonies. Rudy led his wife, his parents, and her parents to the Lord shortly after his own conversion. People were amazed at the changes they saw in Rudy and Douglas. They wanted to know what had changed them. Rudy and Douglas were glad to tell them of the compassion and power of the Lord in their lives. Today Rudy is a pastor in his community.

❖ Spiritual Transformations

This lesson focuses on two miracles of our Lord. Both demonstrate His power and compassion. During a storm on the Sea of Galilee, the disciples asked Jesus if He really cared about them. He showed them He did by stopping the storm. The helpless demoniac was transformed when Jesus cast the demons out of the man's life. Although some people asked Jesus to leave, Jesus told the man to tell his family and friends how the Lord had shown mercy to him.

The Life Impact of this lesson is designed to help us affirm the reality of the Lord's power and compassion for our lives. We need to live in light of His compassion. When we are tempted to doubt that He knows and cares, we need to trust Him. When we are tempted to be silent, we need to tell others how the Lord has shown us His mercy and compassion.

If someone expressed doubt that the Lord knows and cares for that person in life's storms, how would you respond? _____

_____

In what ways have you experienced the Lord's compassion? _____

_____

Prayer of Commitment: Lord, when life becomes stormy, help me to trust in You; when I have opportunities to tell of Your love, help me to bear faithful testimony to You.

[1]Herschel H. Hobbs, *An Exposition of the Gospel of Mark* [Grand Rapids: Baker Book House, 1970], 78.
[2]Anatolius, "On Christ Calming the Sea," in *Divine Inspiration: The Life of Jesus in World Poetry,* edited by Robert Atwan, George Dardess, Peggy Rosenthal [New York: Oxford University Press, 1998], 129.
[3]Hobbs, *An Exposition of the Gospel of Mark,* 81.
[4]Walter W. Wessel, "Mark," in vol. 8 of *The Expositor's Bible Commentary* [Grand Rapids: Zondervan Publishing House, 1984], 658.
[5]Brooks, "Mark," NAC, 91.

GIVING MY ALL

Bible Passage: John 6:1-13
Key Verse: John 6:11

❖ *Significance of the Lesson*

• The *Theme* of this lesson is Jesus is able to do much with only a little when we give it to Him.
• The *Life Question* this lesson seeks to address is Why should I give to Jesus the little bit I have to offer?
• The *Biblical Truth* is that Jesus Christ has the power to take our limited resources and multiply them for His ministry when we give them to Him.
• The *Life Impact* is to help you make yourself, and all you have, available for service to Christ.

Unlimited Needs—Limited Resources

Many adults struggle with how to use their resources. Our materialistic society promotes attitudes of selfishness and self-centeredness. Conscientious adults struggle with how much to give to others and how much to keep for themselves. Some use everything for themselves.

The biblical worldview focuses on giving of ourselves for the Lord and for other people. The Bible challenges all believers to give themselves and their possessions to the Lord. Many have little to give, but the Lord can multiply even a little for the good of many.

The Miracle of Feeding the Five Thousand in the Four Gospels

The feeding of the 5,000 is the only one of Jesus' miracles that is recorded in all four Gospels (Matt. 14:13-21; Mark 6:30-44; Luke 9:10-17; John 6:1-13). This shows its importance. It also shows how distinctively John dealt with it compared to the writers of the Synoptic Gospels. All four Gospels contain the basic facts of the miracle: Jesus was followed by crowds; He used five loaves and two fish to feed five thousand; they had twelve baskets full left.

John's Gospel, however, includes some things not found in Matthew, Mark, or Luke. John alone told of the roles of Philip, Andrew, and the boy. Only John recorded Jesus' mention of not having any waste. However, the most distinctive part of John's account is what followed the feeding of the 5,000. The people tried to make Jesus a king (v. 15). Jesus told the people that they were interested in Him only because He fed them. They failed to see Him as the Bread of life. As a result, "many of his disciples went back, and walked no more with him" (v. 66).

The Number of Passovers and the Length of Jesus' Ministry

The number of Passovers mentioned in John's Gospel is one way to determine the length of Jesus' public ministry. Three seem to be mentioned clearly in John (2:13; 6:4; 12:1). John 5:1 mentions a feast, but does not identify it. If this was a Passover, Jesus' ministry was three-and-one-half years long. If there were only three Passovers, Jesus' ministry was two-and-one-half years long.

Word Study: *Barley loaves*

What do you picture when someone refers to a loaf of bread? In the passage for this week we read about a boy who had five barley loaves and two fish for his lunch. Based on our modern common parlance, some people might think the boy had a huge lunch and would have needed a grocery sack to carry it! Such was not the case. The fish were two small, dried fish (v. 9), and the barley loaves of that day were more like our biscuits. But there is more indicated by the expression *barley loaves,* which only occurs in verses 9 and 13 in the New Testament, than their size. The preferred grain for bread was wheat. Barley was the rough grain used by the poor. The tidbit of fish was designed to make the biscuits more palatable. The poor lad's lunch was a small portion intended for his own consumption.

❖ *Search the Scriptures*

When Jesus and the disciples crossed the Sea of Galilee and went up a mountain, many people followed Him because of the miraculous healings. Jesus asked Philip how the crowd could be fed, and Philip said that two hundred days' wages would not buy enough bread to feed so many. Andrew told Jesus of a small boy who had five barley loaves and two small fish, but wondered how so little would help. After having the people sit on the grass, Jesus took the bread and fish and thanked God. When the food was distributed, all of the 5,000 had all they wanted to eat. Jesus asked the disciples to collect what was left, and there were 12 baskets of food not used.

Test of Faith (John 6:1-6)

Why did so many people follow Jesus across the Sea of Galilee? Why did Jesus ask Philip how they could feed so many people? These questions are addressed in this section.

Verses 1-4: **After these things Jesus went over the sea of Galilee, which is the sea of Tiberias. ²And a great multitude followed him, because they saw his miracles which he did on them that were diseased. ³And Jesus went up into a mountain, and there he sat with his disciples. ⁴And the passover, a feast of the Jews, was nigh.**

After these things is a vague way of describing when the miracle of the feeding of the 5,000 happened. The Synoptic Gospels indicate that it occurred after the mission of the twelve and the death of John the Baptist. Thus it was in the latter half of Jesus' 18-month Galilean ministry. Jesus was looking for a time alone with the disciples to report and rest.

The sea of Galilee was the name of the large lake in and around which so much of Jesus' work was done. Herod Antipas built the city of Tiberias around A.D. 20 and named it for the emperor Tiberius. It was on the south-west part of the body of water. Eventually the lake came to be called **the sea of Tiberias.**

Went over shows that Jesus went from one side of the lake to the other by boat. Most Bible students think that He crossed from the west to the east because later when He went back He was near Capernaum (v. 59), which is on the northwest side. Further, the eastern side of the lake is hill country. On the eastern side of the lake **Jesus went up into a mountain, and there he sat with his disciples.** In that day teachers sat while teaching. Jesus withdrew from the populace on several occasions during the course of His ministry. He needed time away from the crowds to teach His disciples. The indication that **the passover, a feast of the Jews, was nigh** reminds us that only one year of Jesus' earthly ministry remained. It also shows that Jesus did not go to the Passover in Jerusalem that spring.

All four Gospels state that **a great multitude followed him,** probably by walking around the northern end of the lake. John told us that the crowd followed him **because they saw his miracles which he did on them that were diseased.** The word for **miracles** is *semeia,* "signs."

Verses 5-6: **When Jesus then lifted up his eyes, and saw a great company come unto him, he saith unto Philip, Whence shall we buy bread, that these may eat?** [6]**And this he said to prove him: for he himself knew what he would do.**

The arrival of **a great multitude** raised the question of feeding so many people. They had followed Him to a place far from home. Jesus, therefore, asked, **Whence shall we buy bread, that these may eat?** The Synoptic Gospels show that the same question was on the minds of the disciples. Their idea was to send the people away so the people could buy food in nearby villages (Matt. 14:15; Mark 6:35-36; Luke 9:12).

According to John's Gospel, Jesus addressed the question directly to **Philip.** Jesus called **Philip** to follow Him shortly after calling Andrew and Simon Peter (1:43-44). Philip issued an invitation to his friend Nathanael. When Nathanael asked whether any good thing could come out of Nazareth, Philip wisely said, "Come and see" (vv. 45-46). Philip appears twice later in John's Gospel. He was involved when some Greeks came asking if they could see Jesus. Philip took them to Andrew (12:20-22). When Jesus made His famous claim about being the way, the truth, and the life, Philip asked Jesus to show them the Father. Jesus told him that whoever had seen Him had seen the Father (14:6-9).

Prove is *peirazon.* The Greek word can mean either "tempt" or "test." God does not tempt anyone to do evil. He does test our faith to strengthen it. Jesus **himself knew what he would do.** That is, Jesus knew that He would miraculously feed the multitude; but He wanted to test Philip's faith. As Gerald L. Borchert said, "It was not a question for information but a question to probe whether or not Philip understood who Jesus was."[1]

So this was the setting for the miracle. A large multitude, which Matthew 14:21 tells us was about 5,000 men, not counting women and children, needed to be fed. To the twelve, this seemed an impossible task. It is the same way we feel when we consider the many needs and the many needy people in our world. The needs seem unlimited, and we hear calls for help on every side: in church, over television and radio, through mail, by phone, and in daily life. We are people with limited resources in a world of unlimited needs.

These needs include physical needs and spiritual needs. Jesus came primarily to meet spiritual needs, but He practiced and taught meeting all kinds of human needs. Some people focus only on one kind of need. Many of the crowd were following Jesus only because He healed their bodies or fed them. Some people today seem aware only of their physical needs. Jesus, however, called us to give priority to spiritual needs but warned us not to neglect physical needs. In fact, James 2:15-16 calls in question the faith of someone who ignores physical needs. The needs are so great that the temptation is to give up and not do anything.

William Booth, founder of the Salvation Army, was criticized for meeting the physical needs of the poor in London. Those who criticized him said all that mattered was the poor people's souls. Booth replied, "How can you warm a man's heart with the love of Christ when his feet are perishing with cold?"[2]

Responses of Doubt (John 6:7-9)

What can we learn from the responses of Philip and of Andrew? What was the part played by the boy? What is the significance of **little** and of **so many**? These questions are addressed in comments on these verses.

Verses 7-9: **Philip answered him, Two hundred pennyworth of bread is not sufficient for them, that everyone of them may take a little. [8]One of his disciples, Andrew, Simon Peter's brother, saith unto him, [9]There is a lad here, which hath five barley loaves, and two small fishes: but what are they among so many?**

We don't know what vocation **Philip** had before He followed Christ, but his answer to Jesus shows that he could calculate numbers. He apparently had made an estimate of the number of people in the multitude, and he had calculated how much it would cost to feed so many people. Jesus and the twelve apparently had a small amount of money. Judas is said to have held the money bag (12:6). Philip knew that their financial resources were limited.

He had estimated that **two hundred pennyworth of bread** would **not** be **sufficient for them.** This would be true even if each one took only **a little. Pennyworth** translates *denarion.* A denarius was an amount of money equal to a day's wages for a laborer. This is based on the parable of the laborers in Matthew 20:1-16. Translators struggle with how to translate this amount into our language and into today's wages. Translations vary: "eight months' wages" (NIV), "six months' wages" (NRSV), "almost a year's wages" (CEV). Another way to bring it up to date is to multiply two hundred by the current minimum wages for one day. At any rate, this figure represented two hundred days of hard work for working people. Jesus and His disciples probably did not have that much.

Andrew is identified as **Simon Peter's brother.** This reminds us that Andrew had been the one who told his brother about Jesus (1:40-42). Peter became more prominent later. Andrew appears later in John's Gospel when Philip brought to him some Greeks who wanted to see Jesus. Andrew and Philip then took them to Jesus (12:20-22). To Andrew's credit, in each of the three scenes where he appears, he was bringing someone to Jesus. On this occasion, he told Jesus about **a lad** with **five barley loaves, and two small fishes.**

We are not told how Andrew knew this. Probably he had made friends with the boy. **Lad** is *paidarion,* the diminutive form of *pais,* which means "child" or "boy." The diminutive form means "small boy." The **barley loaves** were not the size of today's loaf of bread but more like a roll. Since **barley** was less expensive, the boy was probably from a poor family. **Fishes** translates *opsaria,* which means "tidbit" and does not specify fish per se. However, the other Gospels have *ichthus,* the word for "fish." The boy had two small fish, something like having two sardines.

Although Andrew informed Jesus of the boy and his lunch, the disciple was not optimistic about what could be done for **so many** with so little. **Philip** had used the word **little** (v. 7). He said that they did not have enough for each person to have even **a little.** Now **Andrew** spoke of **so many.** This focuses on the problem as the disciples saw it. The needs were **many,** but they had available only **a little.**

This brings us back to the problem of how we can meet the unlimited needs of our world with limited resources. Just as Philip and Andrew felt they did not have enough for so many people, many Christians feel they do not have enough to give much of their resources to meet what seem to be unlimited needs. As a result, they give little or nothing of their time, talents, and money to help others. At the heart of the issue is a person's understanding of *enough.* We need to have enough to take care of our needs and the needs of our families. The future is uncertain, and we want to be as secure as possible. Philip's and Andrew's view is seen in words such as these: "I don't have enough to do that." "That job is too big for me." "I don't have the time to do this."

The **lad** is a better model of the way of Jesus than the disciples were. All we know about him is what Andrew reported. He had **five barley loaves, and two small fishes.** We are not told anything else about the lad. Was he alone or with relatives or friends? Did he volunteer his lunch to Andrew to be used to help others? Probably he had brought this as his lunch. It ended up in the hands of Jesus, probably because he allowed Jesus to have it. This is the implication of the passage. Andrew surely would not have taken food from a child by force. The lad is typical of all those who give to Jesus what they have. They trust Him to use it to meet needs. When this story is used in a children's Bible study, the lad is pictured as offering his lunch to Andrew and thus to Jesus. Very likely, this is was what happened.

Gloria Fern, International Mission Board missionary to the Philippines, one day saw a group of about 30 street beggars (called *pulubis*) who were hungry, cold, and sick. They sought food and shelter in the wake of an on-coming typhoon. When Gloria went home, she could not get these people off her mind. She asked herself, "How can I sit in my ivory palace and talk strategy for reaching the poor at team meetings and then do nothing for these pulubis during the worst weather we have had?" Therefore, she determined to do what she could. She and her children gathered all their warmest clothes out of their closets. She made a huge pot of noodle soup. She found some large pieces of plastic to be used for shelter. She returned and gave these things to the street people. Based on her experience she wrote, "Pray for these Bajou beggars, for the Christian community to catch a vision, for us to be obedient as God leads us—and for wisdom in helping 5 million other urban poor." Gloria used what she had.

Abundant Provision (John 6:10-13)

What is the significance of Jesus' offering thanks? How could He do so much with so little? What is the significance of the words **as much as they would** and **filled**? These questions are addressed in comments on these verses.

Verses 10-13: **And Jesus said, Make the men sit down. Now there was much grass in the place. So the men sat down, in number about five thousand. [11]And Jesus took the loaves; and when he had given thanks, he distributed to the disciples, and the disciples to them that were set down; and likewise of the fishes as much as they would. [12]When they were filled, he said unto his disciples, Gather up the fragments that remain, that nothing be lost. [13]Therefore they gathered them together, and filled twelve baskets with the fragments of the five barley loaves, which remained over and above unto them that had eaten.**

Jesus had the people to **sit down** on the **grass.** The number of **men** was **about five thousand.** Matthew 14:21 reports there "were about five thousand men, beside woman and children." Then **Jesus took the loaves** and gave **thanks.** Thanks before eating should precede every meal. Jesus had taught the disciples to pray, "Give us day by day our daily bread" (Luke 11:3). Jesus knew that God is the ultimate source of every good thing. The boy had given the bread, but it was ultimately a gift from God.

Jesus **distributed** the bread **to the disciples.** The words **to the disciples** are not in the oldest copies of John and are thus not found in the *Holman Christian Standard Bible.* But they are in Matthew 14:19; Mark 6:41; and Luke 9:16. **The disciples** distributed it **to them that were set down.** Then Jesus did the same thing with the fish.

Notice how the Bible stresses that the people had enough, even more than enough. The key words are **as much as they would ... nothing be lost ... filled.** Jesus' goal was that everyone would have **as much as they would** ("wanted," NIV) and then it states, **they were filled.** After all the people had all they wanted, Jesus told **his disciples** to **gather up the fragments that remain, that nothing be lost.** We are told that the disciples **filled twelve baskets with the fragments.** Each person was **filled,** and so were the **baskets.**

One of Jesus' temptations had been to turn stones into bread (Matt. 4:3). This was not only a personal temptation because He was hungry, but it was also a temptation to fit into the popular expectation of a king who would feed the people and give them prosperity and victory. Jesus refused that temptation in the wilderness and in this passage in verse 15 when the crowds wanted to make Him such a king. As a rule, Jesus was reluctant to become known as one who fulfilled such earthly expectations; however, He fed the 5,000 because He had compassion on them (Matt. 14:14; Mark 6:34).

This was obviously another of Jesus' miracles of power and compassion. Some people have offered a naturalistic explanation for the "miracle." They say that the boy was not the only one who brought a lunch. Others also had food with them. When the boy freely shared his small lunch, others began to share what they had brought. The miracle, as these see it, was the positive effect on others of the boy's generosity. This explanation, however, is not what John intended us to see in the feeding of the 5,000. The lesson John wanted us to see is twofold: (1) Jesus is the Bread of life, of which physical bread is but a sign. This is what Jesus emphasized after the people tried to make Him an earthly king (vv. 14-15, 35-59). (2) Jesus is able to take whatever we give Him and multiply it far beyond anything humanly possible.

The boy's gift was total; he gave all that he had. It showed his generosity toward people and his faith that Jesus would care for him and the others. He was different from the small boy in the old parable who was trying to dig a huge rock out of the ground. His dad saw his efforts and sensed his frustration. He asked, "Have you done all you can do to move the rock?" The boy said that he had. His dad replied, "No, you haven't. You haven't asked me to help."

How can each of us decide which needs the Lord is leading us to meet? We don't have the time, talents, and money to meet all the needs of which we become aware. Therefore we need divine guidance. Sometimes the Lord calls you to meet a need that requires a one-on-one commitment on your part. At other times, we can do our part in meeting needs that require more than one person. In either case, the need can only be met when each believer does his or her part, trusting the Lord to multiply the gifts in ways beyond what we can do. This principle applies to supporting missionary work through the Cooperative Program. We need to be praying, giving, and going.

As in the case of the boy and his lunch, we must exercise generosity, love, and faith. "At the close of life, the question will not be how much have you got, but how much have you given. Not how much have you won, but how much have you done. Not how much have you saved, but how much have you sacrificed. Not how much were you honored, but how much have you served."[3]

❖ Spiritual Transformations

Huge crowds of people followed Jesus because of the miracles of healing that He did. Over 5,000 men and their families followed Him and His disciples to a mountain. To test him, Jesus asked Philip how they could feed the crowd. Philip said that 200 days' wages would not be enough. Andrew told Jesus of a boy with five barley loaves and two small fish, but Andrew did not see how so little could feed so many. Jesus, however, thanked God and then distributed the bread and fish. The people were completely filled and 12 baskets of fragments were collected.

The application of the lesson deals with how Christians are to respond to the seemingly unlimited needs of a hungry and lost world when each of us has only limited resources of time, talents, and money. The answer is for us to give our all—little or much—to the Lord and trust Him to meet our needs and the needs of others.

How do you decide your part in meeting so many needs? _____

_____

If the Lord tested your generosity, faith, and love as He did Philip's, would you pass the test? _____

Prayer of Commitment: Lord, give me wisdom to know what needs I can meet, and help me to act to meet those needs.

[1]Gerald L. Borchert, "John 1–11," in *The New American Commentary,* vol. 25A [Nashville: Broadman & Holman Publishers, 1996], 253.

[2]Quoted in William Barclay, *And He Had Compassion on Them,* 164.

[3]Nathan C. Schaeffer, quoted in *The Speaker's Quote Book,* compiled by Roy B. Zuck [Grand Rapids: Kregel Publications, 1997], 347.

Study Theme

One Solitary Life: The Life Of Jesus

Unit 5: Lord of the Kingdom

Speaking of Jesus as "One Solitary Life," Phillips Brooks said, "All the armies that ever marched, and all the navies that ever were built, and all the parliaments that ever sat, and all the kings that ever reigned, put together have not affected the life of man upon this earth as powerfully as that one solitary life."[1]

This nine-session unit begins with an examination of Jesus' parables of the kingdom. Then it focuses on Peter's confession of Jesus as the Christ, the Son of the living God, and of Jesus' revealing to the disciples the necessity of the cross. After examining the meaning of the transfiguration, the unit's lessons focus on the parable of the good Samaritan, Jesus' teachings on prayer, the parable of the return of the lost son, the raising of Lazarus from the dead, and the rich young man who asked Jesus what he needed to do to inherit eternal life. These events occurred near the end of Jesus' great Galilean ministry, during a time of teaching the disciples in and around Galilee, and in the later Judean and Perean ministries.

This unit is designed to help you
- allow the gospel to bear fruit in your life (Apr. 1).
- live under God's rule (Apr. 8).
- die to self and follow the risen Lord (Apr. 15).
- obey Jesus (Apr. 22).
- demonstrate love toward all people (Apr. 29).
- pray consistently (May 6).
- repent and seek God's forgiveness when you sin (May 13).
- live your life based on and consistent with the eternal life you have received from the One who is the resurrection and the life (May 20).
- give Jesus priority in your life (May 27).

Based on Jesus' parables of the kingdom, what do you know about the kingdom of God? _____

[1]Quoted by Harold A. Bosley, *He Spoke to Them in Parables* [New York: Harper & Row, Publishers, 1963], 16.

RESPONDING TO THE GOSPEL

Background Passage: Matthew 13:1-23
Focal Passage: Matthew 13:1-9,18-23
Key Verse: Matthew 13:8

❖ *Significance of the Lesson*

• The *Theme* of this lesson is people respond to the gospel call in different ways.

• The *Life Question* this lesson seeks to have you answer is What is my response to the gospel?

• The *Biblical Truth* is that the different responses people make to the gospel lead to different results in their lives.

• The *Life Impact* is to help you allow the gospel to bear fruit in your life.

Different Responses to the Gospel

Adults make a variety of responses to the gospel. Some reject or ignore it. Others seem to respond positively, but they soon drift away from the Christian life. Still others seem to have faith, but their lives are filled with worldly things—not the things of God.

The biblical worldview calls for hearing the gospel, receiving it by repentance and faith, and demonstrating the reality of a personal relationship to Christ by bearing fruit in His name.

Jesus' Teaching in Parables

Jesus often used parables in His teaching. Parables often are defined as earthly stories with a heavenly meaning. Parables are different from fables, which use imaginary circumstances. Jesus' parables were taken from life. In many of His parables, He told of a normal life situation but resolved it in an unexpected way (see, for example, Matt. 20:1-16). His parables were like sermon illustrations in story form. Many parables have only one main point; the rest is only the setting for the story, not part of the meaning. Other parables have multiple parts, each of which has meaning. The parable of the sower or soils is such a parable. In one sense, it has one main point: people respond differently to the gospel; then four kinds of responses are illustrated—each of which also has different results.

The Parable of the Sower or the Soils

This parable appears in the three Synoptic Gospels (Matt. 13:3-23; Mark 4:3-25; Luke 8:5-18). It is usually called the parable of the sower; but since the same sower and the same kind of seed are used, it is often called the parable of the soils, of which there were four different kinds. Two basic interpretations of the parable are possible. One interpretation assumes that it was addressed primarily to those who preach the gospel. If so, the basic application is to encourage those who sow the seed of the word not to give up when some hearers reject the message, others seem to hear but prove faithless, and still others never bear positive fruit. The word of encouragement is that some hearers will become true followers and bear fruit for the Lord. The other basic interpretation is addressed to hearers. It challenges hearers to evaluate which of four kinds of hearers they are and to be sure they are bearing fruit for Christ. This lesson will focus on the second basic interpretation.

Word Study: *Parable*

The word *parable* comes from the Greek *parabole*. The basic meaning is a "comparison." In the Old Testament, *parabole* most of the time translates the Hebrew word *mashal*. In the Old Testament *mashal* includes proverbs, similes, allegories, comparisons, and stories. In the New Testament, a parable most often is a story that illustrates something. Some New Testament parables, however, are short stories, proverbs, and sayings.

❖ *Search the Scriptures*

Pressed by large crowds at the shore of the Sea of Galilee, Jesus got into a boat and taught the people using parables. The parable in Matthew 13:3-9 was spoken to the large crowd. The explanation of the parable's meaning in verses 18-23 was given to the disciples alone. For the purposes of this lesson we have grouped the parts of the parable and its explanation together. The parable of the soils is one of several parables in Matthew 13 that explain the polarization of response to Jesus' ministry.

The Hardened Response (Matt. 13:1-4,18-19)

What was the setting for this passage? Why did Jesus teach in parables? What happened to the seed on the path? What kind of people does this soil represent? These questions are addressed in comments on these verses.

Verses 1-4: **The same day went Jesus out of the house, and sat by the seaside. ²And great multitudes were gathered together unto him, so that he went into a ship, and sat; and the whole multitude stood on the shore. ³And he spake many things unto them in parables, saying, Behold, a sower went forth to sow; ⁴and when he sowed, some seeds fell by the wayside, and the fowls came and devoured them up.**

The events of Matthew 12 and the teaching of chapter 13 are closely related. This is seen in the fact that they happened on **the same day.** Both chapters describe a growing difference in positive and negative responses to Jesus. **The house** probably refers to the house mentioned in Matthew 8:14; 9:10,28. As was often true in Jesus' life, **great multitudes** followed Him. Jesus **went into a ship** ("boat," NIV) and using it as His platform from there **spake many things unto them in parables.** Chapter 13 includes eight parables, all related to the kingdom of heaven. The parable in verses 3-9 was spoken to the multitude and was later explained to His disciples in verses 18-23. Verses 10-17 explain why Jesus so often used parables.

Most of Jesus' parables were based on everyday life in first-century lands of the Jews. Since theirs was basically a rural society, Jesus began this group of parables with a familiar sight—**a sower went forth to sow.** The word **behold** shows that this was to be more than just a story about a farmer sowing his crop.

In those days farmers broadcast their **seeds.** That is, they cast seeds over a broad area. Like all farmers, their goal was to use the maximum amount of the precious land for growing crops. So they tried to plow most of it. However, they had to have a path along which they walked. They tried to avoid tramping down too much of the field, but some of it became hard. As the sower threw out his seeds, some fell **by the wayside. Wayside** means "path" (NIV). **By** is *para*, which usually means "along side of," but here may include "on" (NRSV).

The seeds lay in full view. The path was too hard for the seeds to take root. Luke 8:5 says the seeds were "trodden down." Thus **the fowls** ("birds," NIV) **came and devoured them up** ("ate it up," NIV).

Verses 18-19: **Hear ye therefore the parable of the sower. ¹⁹When anyone heareth the word of the kingdom, and understandeth it not, then**

cometh the wicked one, and catcheth away that which was sown in his heart. This is he which received seed by the wayside.

Hear is a key word in the Bible in general and in this passage in particular. Jesus called this **the parable of the sower.** There is one sower in the parable and his sowing is crucial to the story, just as there is one kind of seed. The differences are in the kinds of soil. Therefore, it also can be called the parable of the soils. As noted earlier, this parable has two possible basic interpretations. One sees it as applying to those who sow the seed of **the word of the kingdom.** The other emphasizes the word **hear,** which appears throughout the parable, and sees it as applying to all who hear the word.

The word of the kingdom is the same as the "gospel of the kingdom" (Matt. 4:23). The parallel passages have "word" (Mark 4:16) and "the word of God" (Luke 8:11). In the Synoptic Gospels, **kingdom** is a key word. It refers to the reign of God first in people's hearts and someday over all things. When the disciples asked Jesus why He spoke in parables, He said, "Because it is given unto you to know the mysteries of the kingdom of heaven, but to them it is not given" (Matt. 13:11). Thus only by faith do the meanings of the parables become clear.

The seed that fell on the path represents what happens **when anyone heareth the word of the kingdom, and understandeth it not. Understandeth** (*sunientos*) is a key word in the parable. The Greek word was used to refer to more than an intellectual understanding. This is especially true when it is used with **heart. Heart** is *kardia*, which meant more to them than it does to us. For us, when the word *heart* is used of something more than the organ, it refers to emotions. In the Bible, the heart is the seat of physical, mental, and spiritual life. The key to the meaning of **understandeth** in this parable is in verses 13-15, which in turn is a quotation from Isaiah 6:9-10.

> For this people's heart has become calloused;
>> they hardly hear with their ears,
>> and they have closed their eyes (v. 15, NIV).

In other words, the problem was not just a failure of the mind to understand the word of the kingdom; it also was a matter of their rejecting that word. The rejection can be manifested in violent rejection of Jesus or in ignoring the call to receive Him.

The birds that ate the seed represent **the wicked one** (the parallel passage in Luke 8:12 has "the devil"). He **catcheth away** ("snatches away," NIV) **that which was sown in** the person's **heart.** The devil is always diligently at work to thwart the effectiveness of God's Word. Paul wrote, "The god of this age has blinded the minds of unbelievers, so that they cannot see the light of the gospel of the glory of Christ, who is the image of God" (2 Cor. 4:4, NIV). This does not mean that unbelievers can blame their unbelief on the devil. It means, however, that if people choose to reject of ignore the Word of God, Satan works to further harden their hearts.

People who reject the gospel of Jesus do so in a variety of ways. Nevertheless, when they harden their hearts, their hearts became even harder. When they refuse the light, they go deeper into spiritual darkness.

The Superficial Response (Matt. 13:5-6,20-21)

What is meant by **stony places**? What kind of hearers are described here? Were they believers who turned away from Christ? These questions are addressed in comments on these verses.

Verses 5-6: **Some fell upon stony places, where they had not much earth: and forthwith they sprung up, because they had no deepness of earth: ⁶And when the sun was up, they were scorched; and because they had no root, they withered away.**

Stony places does not refer to ground littered with many rocks; it means soil that is over a ledge of rock that is just under a thin layer of soil. Luke 8:6 has "upon a rock." This is the reason these seeds **had not much earth** ("the soil was shallow," NIV). **They had no deepness of earth** because of the ledge of rock. Therefore, the seed that fell into such soil quickly **sprung up**. There was much of this kind of soil in the land.

When **the sun** rose, the tender shoots **were scorched; and because they had no root, they withered away.** Luke 8:6 adds, "because it lacked moisture." Many of Jesus' hearers probably were farmers. If so, they were familiar with what He described.

Verses 20-21: **But he that received the seed into stony places, the same is he that heareth the word, and anon with joy receiveth it; ²¹yet hath he not root in himself, but endureth for a while: for when tribulation or persecution ariseth because of the word, by and by he is offended.**

This kind of soil represents the person **that heareth the word, and anon with joy receiveth it.** To all appearances, such people had a genuine religious experience. Notice these characteristics: (1) They acted **anon** ("at once," NIV; "immediately," NRSV) and did not postpone their decision. (2) They received the word (**receiveth it**). Receiving the word is the proper response when people hear the word of God. (3) They did this **with joy.** This is also a mark of genuine faith (see Acts 8:8).

Verse 21 shows the deadly characteristics of this response. Such a person **hath he not root in himself** ("he has no root," NIV). Because of this, **he endureth for a while. For a while** is *proskairos,* it means "lasting only a short time," "temporary," "transitory."

Superficial hearers last only until they experience **tribulation or persecution.** These troubles and opposition come upon them **because of the word.** **Tribulation** is *thlipseos,* it comes from *thlibo,* which means "to press," "to oppress," or "to squeeze." It refers to a wide variety of troubles that press in on people. The word **persecution** is *diogmou.* The root meaning is "to run" or "to press on." It also came to mean "to persecute."

By and by translates *euthus,* which means "quickly" (NIV) or "immediately" (NRSV). This same word is used in both verses 20 and 21. When they heard the gospel, they immediately received the word with joy; however, when the gospel brings trouble or persecution, they just as quick are **offended.** The verb translated **offended** is *skandalizetai.* It can refer to being "offended" or it can mean "falls away" (NIV, NASB, NRSV). The latter is more likely here.

This kind of hearer is the one who makes what appears to be a genuine profession of faith, even an especially quick and joyful one. Yet when trouble comes, these people turn away from following Jesus. Some go so far as to renounce their former faith, or they simply cease to practice the Christian faith.

Pliny the Younger was governor of Bithynia in the early second century. Some of his letters to Trajan, the Roman emperor, have been preserved. These letters give insight into the situation in the early days of persecution. In one of these letters Pliny wrote Trajan and described his way of dealing with professing Christians. Pliny did not go looking for Christians; however, if people were accused of being Christians, he brought them to trial. He asked if they were Christians. Those who said they were Christians were told that they would be executed if they continued to follow Christ. They were given three opportunities to turn from Christ. They demonstrated this by cursing Christ and participating in worshiping the emperor. Pliny wrote that cursing Christ was "a thing which, it is said, genuine Christians cannot be induced to do." When this approach was used on people accused of being Christians, many went to their deaths rather than curse Christ, but some "said that they were Christians and then denied it; declaring that they had been but were so no longer, some having recanted three years or more before and one or two as long as twenty years."[1]

Those who renounced Christ were like the seed that fell on shallow soil. They professed faith in Christ, but later they renounced their faith. This kind of persecution is still a reality in many countries of the world. Most American Christians have not faced life-or-death persecution. Yet our church rolls are filled with the names of people who once made a profession of faith and joined the church but now are living in ways that deny Christ.

The initial profession of some people is like a fireworks display—it is emotional and dramatic. Many of these people are dedicated Christians, but some no longer darken the door of the church. They live no differently from non-Christians. Some live openly shameful lives. How can this be? How can a true Christian do such things?

Those of us who believe in eternal security for those who truly are saved also believe in both the preservation of the saints and the perseverance of the saints. God preserves those who belong to Him; one evidence of this is that they persevere in faithfulness. A profession of faith in Christ is not the only evidence of salvation. Some people make a profession that is later called in question by their sinful actions (see Matt. 7:21). Some of these people may be seriously backslidden believers, but others of them never truly were saved. Their profession seemed to be genuine, but their later actions showed that they had no real root to start with.

The Divided Response (Matt. 13:7,22)

How is this response different from and like the first two? Are such people true believers who fail to bear good fruit, or are they unsaved people? These questions are addressed in comments on these verses.

Verses 7,22: **And some fell among thorns; and the thorns sprung up, and choked them. . . . ²²He also that received seed among the thorns is he that heareth the word; and the care of this world, and the deceitfulness of riches, choke the word, and he becometh unfruitful.**

The third kind of hearers were those like seeds that **fell among thorns.** These were probably in the corners of the fields. The seed was not on a hard path, nor was the soil shallow. The soil was deep enough for the seed to have a root. What then was the problem? The plants grew up **among thorns,** which **sprung up, and choked them.** Mark 4:7 says, "The thorns grew up, and choked it, and it yielded no fruit."

Like the seed sown in shallow soil, the seed sown among thorns pictures people who hear **the word,** but **the care of this world, and the deceitfulness of riches, choke the word, and** they become **unfruitful. Care** is *merimna,* which refers to anxieties or worries. Jesus used this word in His warning against being anxious concerning such physical things as food and clothing (Matt. 6:25-34). Worldly concern will hinder the fruitfulness of one who has heard the word of God. Anxieties about worldly things are marks of allegiance to the world.

Deceitfulness is *apate,* which can mean either "deceitfulness" (KJV, NASB, NIV) or "delight." The *Holman Christian Standard Bible* goes with "the pleasure of wealth." The *New Revised Standard Version* has "the lure of wealth." Both meanings are true of those who allow wealth to become too much of their lives. Riches are deceitful because they promise more than they can deliver. They lure to destruction people who seek to become rich and to cling to their wealth (see 1 Tim. 6:17). Jesus warned that no one can worship God and mammon (Matt. 6:24). He told the parable of the rich fool, who was lured to destruction by his preoccupation with becoming financially secure (Luke 12:16-21).

The word **unfruitful** is *akarpos. Karpos* is "fruit." The letter *a* stands for "not" or the prefix "un." Are those of this third group true believers? Bible students debate about whether Jesus intended the seed among thorns to represent true Christians who fail to bear fruit or people who never really knew Christ. Those who consider them lost point to the fact that they never bore fruit for the Lord. Bearing evil fruit is surely a mark of the unsaved (Matt. 12:35-36), but bearing no good fruit is also condemned (Luke 13:6-9; John 15:1-11). Herschel H. Hobbs took the view they were true Christians. He wrote: "Such receive the **word,** and it takes root and grows. These are genuine believers. But they are those who fall short of a full commitment to Christ."[2] On the other hand, Craig L. Blomberg, writing in the *New American Commentary,* concluded: "The first three kinds of soils are all inadequate. None of them stands for people who were ever true believers, despite certain outward appearances."[3]

This should a sobering passage for that vast host of church members who bear no fruit for the Lord.

The Genuine Response (Matt. 13:8-9,23)

Why is hearing **the word** such a responsibility? What did Jesus mean by **fruit**? What kind of person is represented by the **good ground**? These questions are addressed in comments on these verses.

Verses 8-9: **But other fell into good ground, and brought forth fruit, some an hundredfold, some sixtyfold, some thirtyfold. [9]Who hath ears to hear, let him hear.**

Good ground is soil that is not too hard to receive the seed, not too shallow for the seed to have roots, and not so choked by thorns that it cannot bear fruit. It is the plowed part of the field that receives the seed, which sinks its roots into it, and grows to maturity bearing fruit in its season. Such seed **brought forth fruit.** Some had fruit that was **an hundredfold, some sixtyfold, some thirtyfold.** The differences probably represent differences in gifts and in capacity for bearing fruit—like the differences in the number of talents entrusted to each of the servants in the parable of the talents (Matt. 25:14-30). Each faithful steward was commended for having done his best.

Verse 9 is a summary verse that applies to all who hear the word of the kingdom—**Who hath ears to hear, let him hear.** In the Bible, to truly **hear** is to obey. J. H. Jowett was a powerful preacher in his day. A member of the congregation was boasting to a friend that he heard Dr. Jowett each Sunday. His friend surprised him by saying, "What a terrible responsibility!"[4] Many people try to avoid hearing the word of the Lord. This evasion of the word does not excuse them from their responsibility.

Verse 23: **But he that received seed into the good ground is he that heareth the word, and understandeth it; which also beareth fruit, and bringeth forth, some an hundredfold, some sixty, some thirty.**

The person represented by the fourth kind of soil is the kind of person all should be. This person not only **hearth the word** but also **understandeth it.** Remember that **understandeth** in this parable means more than intellectual understanding. It refers to someone who believes and commits to the Lord. Luke 8:15 reads, "That on the good ground are they, which in an honest and good heart, having heard the word, keep it, and bring forth fruit with patience." Thus **understandeth** is with the heart and the will. As a result, this person is the only one of the four who bears fruit for the Lord.

What did Jesus mean by **fruit**? I recall a seminar in which there was a lively debate about the meaning. Some insisted that fruit referred to other Christians who are won to Christ by the person's witness. The other side maintained that fruit was the quality of Christian living. Actually both of these kinds of fruit receive priority in the teachings of the New Testament. The word **fruit** is used of both. Paul wrote to the Roman believers saying that he wanted to visit them so that he might have some fruit among them (Rom. 1:13). This is reinforced by his words in verses 14-16. On the other hand, many passages use the word **fruit** to refer to Christlike living. The most familiar is probably Paul's reference in Galatians 5:22 to the fruit of the Spirit. Both kinds of fruit—winning others to Christ and living a Christlike life—are expected of those who truly hear the word of God.

❖ *Spiritual Transformations*

The parable of the soils describes four kinds of responses to the word of the kingdom, each of which represents a different kind of hearer. The seed on the hard path represents those who never allow the word to sprout. The seed on shallow soil represents those who hear the word, seem to make a genuine profession of faith, but soon turn away from the Lord because of troubles. The seed among thorns represents people who never bear fruit for the Lord. The seed on good ground represents those who hear and heed the word, thus bearing fruit for the Lord.

This parable challenges us to hear the word of God, to open our hearts to it, and to bear fruit for the Lord. Bearing fruit is the crucial test of whether we have truly done this. Just making a profession of faith is not the sole criterion for determining how genuine our profession is. The kind of fruit we bear is the primary test.

Which of the four kinds of hearers are you? _____

_____

What kind of fruit does your life have? _____

_____

Prayer of Commitment: Lord, help me to hear Your word in my heart and to bear fruit for Your glory.

[1]Pliny the Younger, *Epp. X (ad Traj.)*, xcvi, in *Documents of the Christian Church*, edited by Bettenson, 6.

[2]Herschel H. Hobbs, *An Exposition of the Gospel of Matthew*, [Grand Rapids: Baker Book House, 1965], 170.

[3]Craig L. Blomberg, "Matthew," in *The New American Commentary*, vol. 22 [Nashville: Broadman Press, 1992], 214.

[4]Quoted by Leslie D. Weatherhead, *In Quest of a Kingdom* [Nashville: Abingdon-Cokebury Press, 1944], 195.

LIVING UNDER GOD'S RULE

Background Passage: Matthew 13:24-52
Focal Passage: Matthew 13:31-35,44-52
Key Verse: Matthew 13:52

❖ *Significance of the Lesson*

• The *Theme* of this lesson is Jesus taught about the kingdom in parables.
• The *Life Question* this lesson seeks to address is How is God at work in the world today?
• The *Biblical Truth* is that the kingdom of heaven involves God's often unseen but powerful activity to accomplish His purposes and extend His rule.
• The *Life Impact* is to help you live under God's rule.

Adults and the Kingdom of Heaven

Many adults resist any person or power ruling them. Our American heritage encourages freedom from kings and lords. Some adults apply this to God as King. Some do not believe in God, and of those who do believe He exists, may live without any personal relationship with Him.

In the biblical worldview God is King, and He has declared His sovereignty in Jesus Christ. God is at work in the world today to bring in His kingdom. People are to open their lives to His rule. This begins with repentance and faith in Jesus Christ; and it leads to living, praying, and witnessing in the light of God's eternal kingdom.

Parables of the Kingdom

Matthew 13 contains eight parables, all of which present some earthly thing that represents truths concerning the kingdom of heaven. None of these parables is very long, but two of the parables are longer than the others. Jesus also explained these two—the parable of the sower and the parable of the wheat and tares. The other six parables are short comparisons of some truth about the kingdom of heaven to some earthly experience. These six short parables are the biblical content for this lesson.

Word Study: *Kingdom of heaven*

Basileia is the Greek word for "kingdom." The word can refer to a realm over which a king rules, or it can refer to the reign of the king. The expression "kingdom of heaven," which is found 33 times and only in Matthew, means the same as "the kingdom of God." For the Jews, who avoided using God's name, "heaven" often was used to refer to God.

The Bible teaches that the sovereign reign of God is past, present, and future. The eternal God has always been King, whether or not people recognized Him as Ruler. Jesus Christ came to open the way to the kingdom through His life, death, and resurrection. Thus He declared that the kingdom was present in Him (Luke 11:20), but its consummation is yet future (v. 2).

Responses to the Kingdom

We do not build the kingdom of God; only God can do that. We can enter the kingdom by acknowledging the lordship of Jesus Christ. We can bear witness to the reality of the kingdom, and thus seek to extend the kingdom. We can live our earthly lives in light of the eternal kingdom (Matt. 5:3-12). We can give priority to the things of the kingdom (6:33). We can pray for the coming of the kingdom (v. 10).

❖ *Search the Scriptures*

The parables of the mustard seed and the leaven teach how the kingdom grows from small, insignificant beginnings. Much of this growth is unseen. The parables of the hidden treasure and the pearl of great price illustrate the supreme worth of the kingdom. The kingdom is far more valuable than anything given up to enter it. The parable of the net warns of the judgment of those who reject the kingdom. The parable of the householder calls disciples to disciple others with the treasures that result from becoming a disciple of Jesus.

Kingdom Growth (Matt. 13:31-35)

In what way is the kingdom of heaven like a **mustard seed**? In what way is it like **leaven**? How is the growth of the kingdom revealed? What did Matthew mean by saying that Jesus taught only in parables? How did this fulfill Psalm 78:2? These questions are addressed in the following comments on these verses.

Verses 31-32: **Another parable put he forth unto them, saying, The kingdom of heaven is like a grain of mustard seed, which a man took, and sowed in his field:** [32]**which indeed is the least of all seeds: but when it is grown, it is the greatest among herbs, and becometh a tree, so that the birds of the air come and lodge in the branches thereof.**

This is the third parable in Matthew 13, and each of the three tells of someone sowing seed. In the parable of the soils, the emphasis in on the different kinds of hearers of God's word. In the parable of the wheat and the tares, the emphasis is on judgment being postponed until the end. In the parable of the **mustard seed,** the sower planted only one seed. The point is that the kingdom grows from small beginnings.

The **mustard seed** is called the **least of all seeds** ("the smallest of all the seeds," NRSV, HCSB). As the *New International Version*'s rendering indicates ("the smallest of all your seeds"), Jesus may have meant that it was the smallest seed used in Palestine. The small size of **a grain of mustard seed** was proverbial in that land. Jesus was not speaking as a botanist but as a teacher, who used what was known by His hearers. The point is that the kingdom had what appeared to have a small, insignificant beginning.

This tiny seed grows; and **when it is grown, it is the greatest among herbs, and becometh a tree.** A mustard seed grows into a large bush. It's like a **tree** because **birds** build their nests in it. Some Bible students see the **birds** as representing something other than birds, that is, the vast number of Gentiles who would later come to Christ. Probably the birds are mentioned only to show the size of the grown plant. Thus the point is that the kingdom grows to be what God wants it to be, but it grows from seemingly insignificant beginnings.

When Jesus came, many Jews expected a spectacular kingdom that would immediately return them to the kind of prominence that Israel had in the days of David and Solomon. This parable corrected that false idea.

It takes a while for the tiny seed to grow to maturity. So does the kingdom of heaven take time—God's time. Gene Mims wrote: "The kingdom of God is not geographical, political, or social. It knows no human or earthly limits; neither does it depend on human effort. God has chosen to involve you and me in the advance of His kingdom, but His kingdom rests on His power, not ours."[1]

Verse 33: **Another parable spake he unto them; The kingdom of heaven is like unto leaven, which a woman took, and hid in three measures of meal, till the whole was leavened.**

Jesus then compared **the kingdom of heaven** to **leaven** ("yeast," NIV, HCSB). *Zume* was a common item in Jewish households. Thus women could relate to this parable as the men could to the parables about sowing. In most biblical references to **leaven,** it symbolizes something evil. Because of this, it was to be purged from Jewish households at Passover (Ex. 12:15,19). Jesus warned against "the leaven of the scribes and Pharisees" (Matt. 16:6,11-12). Paul used **leaven** to signify an evil person or influence to be avoided (1 Cor. 5:6; Gal. 5:9). Because of this identification of leaven with evil, some Bible students look for that meaning in Matthew 13:33. However, Jesus used **leaven** positively here.

The emphasis here is that a little **leaven** spreads throughout the dough and causes it to rise. The **leaven** was **hid in three measures of meal.** This was enough grain to feed well over 100 people. The **leaven** thus illustrates another kind of growth from the **mustard seed.** Both illustrate how the kingdom grows large from small beginnings, but the seed's growth into the tree is easier to observe than the hidden working of the **leaven.**

How is the growth of the kingdom demonstrated? In one sense, we can see it in numbers of people won to Christ and in changed lives. Yet the ultimate growth of the kingdom is not the size of a church or a denomination or in any statistical way of measuring success. The full growth and expansion of the kingdom will be revealed in the future consummation of God's redemptive work.

Three basic truths are taught in these two parables: (1) The kingdom has small, seemingly insignificant beginnings. (2) It grows by the power of God in ways often unseen by human beings. (3) It grows slowly until it reaches its full growth.

Verses 34-35: **All these things spake Jesus unto the multitude in parables; and without a parable spake he not unto them:** [35]**that it might be fulfilled which was spoken by the prophet, saying, I will open my mouth in parables; I will utter things which have been kept secret from the foundation of the world.**

These verses are like verses 10-18; that is, they refer to all the parables. To whom did Jesus speak the parables? He spoke many of them **unto the multitude,** but He gave some only to the disciples and He explained them to the disciples (vv. 2,36). The words **without a parable spake he not unto them** apparently are in reference to His teachings in that setting, for parables were not Jesus' only way of teaching. Verse 35 quotes Psalm 78:2 as pointing to this teaching by using parables. The obvious truth here is that Jesus often used stories in His teaching. People of all ages can remember stories better than concepts without stories.

Kingdom Worth (Matt. 13:44-46)

How is the kingdom like a hidden treasure? How is it like a pearl of great price? How are the two parables in verses 44-46 alike and how are they different?

Verse 44: Again, the kingdom of heaven is like unto treasure hid in a field; the which when a man hath found, he hideth, and for joy thereof goeth and selleth all that he hath, and buyeth that field.

Treasure hid in a field was not uncommon in the time of Jesus. People often hid their valuables in a hole in the ground (see Matt. 25:25). Some unknown person had buried this treasure. We are not told who or why.

A man probably was a workman, who was plowing a field and **found** the **treasure** by chance—since nothing is indicated about him looking for treasure. The fact that he had to buy the field shows that he was not on his own property. When he found the treasure, he re-hid it—apparently in the same place where he had found it. We are not told why he didn't report the discovery to the owner of the land, try to locate who buried it, take it to some other place, or why he left it where he would have to use all his resources to buy the field to have the treasure. Apparently Jesus' original hearers were more aware of the laws and customs of that day. Further, we should remember that Jesus' parables did not always depict good people. In His parables Jesus did not always use people as examples of how to act but as part of a story that makes a point. As Blomberg pointed out, "We need neither justify his behavior nor imitate it. This is simply part of the story line that helps to make sense of the plot."[2]

He was so anxious to have the treasure for himself that he sold all he had to have enough to purchase the field. We are not told what the treasure was, but the man felt it was worth all he had. The treasure was something so valuable to him that he joyfully gave up everything to have it.

The point Jesus was making was that the kingdom of heaven is of supreme value. Whatever we may give up to have the treasure is worth the price. In one sense receiving the kingdom is free, yet in another sense it is costly. Repentance sometimes involves giving up some cherished things or activities. Those who have found the **joy** of the kingdom testify that they have gained far more than they gave up. This was Paul's testimony in Philippians 3:4-11.

Verses 45-46: Again, the kingdom of heaven is like unto a merchant man, seeking goodly pearls: [46]who, when he had found one pearl of great price, went and sold all that he had, and bought it.

A merchant is *emporo*, which "denotes not a mere shopkeeper, but one who travels to procure what he sells."[3] Thus he was **seeking goodly pearls.**

Pearls were especially prized in that time. While this merchant was looking for quality pearls, he **found one pearl of great price.** *Polutimon* means "of great value" (NIV) or "priceless" (HCSB). The man who had been seeking good pearls had found one of supreme value, so valuable that he **sold all that he had** so he might buy that one pearl.

The two parables emphasize the supreme value of the kingdom of heaven. The workman found the **treasure** by accident. The **merchant** found the **pearl** while he was looking for pearls. Both recognized they had found something more valuable than all they possessed. Therefore, they used all their other resources to gain that thing of ultimate value. Their actions must have made them seem foolish or crazy to their friends. What could be so valuable to do that?

Jesus' answer is that people should "seek . . . first the kingdom of God, and his righteousness" (Matt. 6:33). Later in His ministry, Jesus met a rich man who seemed interested in entering the kingdom (19:16-22). When Jesus called him to sell everything and give the proceeds to the poor, the man refused. Those who enter the kingdom discover the same truth that the two people in these parables discovered.

Russell Conwell, the famous preacher and founder of Temple University, began his book *Acres of Diamonds* by telling of a man living in South Africa during the time of "diamond fever" when people were madly seeking diamonds. The man sold his home and searched for diamonds, but found none. To his dismay, years later he discovered that his old dwelling had been over what was the largest diamond mine. He is typical of the many who fail to recognize in Jesus Christ the pearl of great price.

Augustine, like Paul, recognized the value of what he had in Christ. As he related in his *Confessions,* he struggled for a long time, being unwilling to part with the delights of his life of sin. Then he found that the delights of knowing Christ far surpassed any of the passing deadly delights of life apart from the Lord.

These two parables emphasize the supreme value of the kingdom. Receiving it is costly, but it is of far greater value than anything given up to enter it. Some find the kingdom while seeking it; some have it revealed while they were not seeking it.

Kingdom Judgment (Matt. 13:47-50)

How is the parable of the net like the parable of the tares? how is it different? What is the main teaching of the parable of the net? These questions are addressed in comments on these verses.

Verses 47-50: Again, the kingdom of heaven is like unto a net, that was cast into the sea, and gathered of every kind: [48]which, when it was full, they drew to shore, and sat down, and gathered the good into vessels, but cast the bad away. [49]So shall it be at the end of the world: the angels shall come forth, and sever the wicked from among the just, [50]and shall cast them into the furnace of fire: there shall be wailing and gnashing of teeth.

Net is *sagene*, which was a "dragnet" (NASB). A large net had weights on the bottom so that it could be dragged along the bottom. Two boats held either end of the net, and they dragged it toward **shore.** The purpose was to trap all the fish in the area through which the net was pulled. When they did this, they **gathered of every kind.** They separated the fish. **The good** fish were placed in **vessels** ("baskets," NIV, NRSV; "containers," NASB, HCSB). **The bad** fish were discarded. **Bad** is *sapra*, which means "rotten." These fish were unfit to eat.

This is the only one of the last six parables that Jesus explained. He said that the separation of the good fish from the bad fish would take place **at the end of the world.** The instruments of this judgment will be **the angels.** They **shall come forth, and sever the wicked from among the just** ("righteous," NIV). The **wicked** shall then be **cast . . . into the furnace of fire.** The words **wailing and gnashing of teeth** show that Jesus was referring to hell.

This parable is like the parable of the tares (vv. 24-30,36-43) in that both teach the certainty of coming judgment. However, the parable of the tares gives more emphasis to the time before judgment when the righteous and unrighteous are together. Bible students have disagreed about where Jesus meant that the wicked and the righteous are together. Some people argue that the good and the bad are together in the church. They emphasize that Jesus said the **wicked** would be separated **from among the just.** We believe Jesus was talking about good and bad people in the world, for He said, "The field is the world" (v. 38).

This is not to deny that there are some unregenerate people who are church members; however, it is to stress that the judgment will include all people. This judgment will be a reality, and so will the eternal punishment of the wicked. Thus how one responds to the kingdom is of great significance. Refusing to enter the kingdom is rejecting the only One who can save from sin and bring eternal life. This parable says nothing about the heavenly life of those who enter the kingdom, but other passages do. The emphasis here is on warning of the ultimate consequences of one's response to the kingdom of heaven.

This parable and the parable of the tares show that the kingdom that was revealed in Jesus' first coming was primarily for salvation, but the future aspect of salvation will include judgment. God's purpose is to save, but judgment is inevitable on those who reject salvation.

Thus the message of the parable of the net is this: (1) Judgment is coming. (2) The righteous shall be separated from the wicked. (3) The wicked shall be sent to hell.

Kingdom Treasures (Matt. 13:51-52)

Did the disciples fully understand? What are the meanings of the words **scribe, instructed,** and **treasure**? What is the meaning and application of the parable of the **householder**? These questions are addressed by comments on these verses.

Verses 51-52: **Jesus saith unto them, Have ye understood all these things? They say unto him, Yea, Lord.** [52]**Then said he unto them, Therefore every scribe which is instructed unto the kingdom of heaven is like unto a man that is an householder, which bringeth forth out of his treasure things new and old.**

When Jesus asked the disciples if they **understood,** they said they did. **Understood** is the same word so prominent in the early part of the chapter (see vv. 14,19,23). By saying they understood, the disciples were claiming to be among those who received the seed of the word, understood, and were bearing fruit for the Lord. We know from later passages that their understanding of the way of the cross was still immature, but they did understand what Jesus had taught them about the parables. This was a foundation for the fuller understanding to which Christ was leading them. This understanding was the foundation for the parable of the **householder.**

Verse 52 has been translated, interpreted, and applied in a variety of ways. Let's begin by defining key words. The word **scribe** is *grammateus*, which is used mostly in the New Testament to refer to the experts in studying, interpreting, and applying the Jewish law. The scribes generally opposed Jesus. Jesus, however, used the word here of His followers. He wanted His followers to be as knowledgeable of the Word of God as any of the Jewish scribes.

Instructed is *matheteutheis.* The word means "to make disciples." This word is in the Great Commission (28:19). Disciples are to make disciples of others.

Treasure is *thesaurou*, the same word used in 2:11 of what the wise men brought to the child Jesus. It is also the word used in 6:19-20 of treasures on earth or in heaven. It can refer to the treasure itself or to the place where the treasure is kept.

Based on these definitions, the verse can be translated, "Every student of the Scriptures who becomes a disciple in the kingdom of heaven is like someone who brings out new and old treasures from the storeroom" (CEV).

As disciples grow in knowledge and experience, they store up truths from God's Word. Jesus calls us to share these treasures with others.

What is the significance of some treasures being **new** and some being **old**? Perhaps Jesus had in mind the foundation of the Old Testament and the revelation of the New Testament. The old may be the eternal God and the new His revelation in Christ. The old represented foundational truths about God, on which the new covenant was built.

Jesus, therefore, was emphasizing several truths: Jesus made disciples of the twelve. They in turn were to make disciples of others. Disciples ought to be proficient in their knowledge of the Word of God. They are to share the new and old treasures from their storehouse of knowledge and experience.

❖ Spiritual Transformations

In his Gettysburg Address, Lincoln referred to the United States as a nation "under God." Years later these words were added to the Pledge of Allegiance to the American flag. This avoids the trap of identifying our nation with the kingdom of God, yet it affirms several things: No earthly nation is the kingdom of God. A nation in which people of faith seek to worship and serve God is a nation that recognizes that we are under the eternal rule of God. Each of us lives under the rule of God.

The parables in Matthew 13 illustrate some of what it means to live "under God." The last six parables teach: (1) The kingdom of heaven had small beginnings by earthly standards, but it is growing; and by God's power and in God's time, its full growth will be revealed. (2) People of faith realize that their relationship to the Lord is the most valuable thing they have. (3) When God's kingdom comes at the end of the age, judgment is sure on the wicked. (4) Christian disciples should disciple others by sharing the riches of what is found in Christ.

How does your life bear witness to the value you attach to the kingdom of God? _____

What does it mean to you to live "under God"? _____

_____

Prayer of Commitment: Lord, help me to live my life by the values of Your eternal kingdom.

[1]Gene Mims, *Kingdom Principles for Church Growth* [Nashville: Convention Press, 1994], 12.
[2]Blomberg, "Matthew," NAC, 223.
[3]John A. Broadus, *A Commentary on the Gospel of Matthew,* in The American Commentary [Philadelphia: American Baptist Publication Society, 1886], 305.

CONFESSING CHRIST

Bible Passage: Matthew 16:13-28
Key Verse: Matthew 16:16

❖ *Significance of the Lesson*

• The *Theme* of this lesson is Jesus is the Christ.
• The *Life Question* this lesson seeks to address is Who do I think Jesus is?
• The *Biblical Truth* is that Jesus is the Son of God who died, was raised on the third day, and calls His followers to a life of self-sacrifice and self-denial.
• The *Life Impact* is to help you die to self and follow the risen Lord.
• This is the *Easter: Coordinated Evangelism Lesson.*

Varying Answers to Who Jesus Is

Adults give a variety of answers to who Jesus is. The negative answers range all the way from strong rejection to appreciation that falls short of true faith. Many people accept the fact that Jesus was a great man and teacher, who affected human history in significant ways. Some profess to believe in Him as Savior, but they do not live as committed disciples of His.

The biblical worldview understands Jesus as the eternal Son of God, who came to earth to reveal God and to redeem sinners from death unto life. His coming, life, teachings, death, and resurrection show that He was more than a prophet or great teacher. Belief in Him involves commitment to the way of the cross and resurrection in our living as well as in our worship and beliefs.

A Watershed Passage

Matthew 16:13-28 is one of the most important passages in the Gospel of Matthew for at least four reasons: (1) It contains the first clear confession of the disciples' faith in the Gospel of Matthew. (2) It contains the first mention of the church in the Gospels. (3) It contains the first prediction by Jesus of His coming death and resurrection. (4) It contains the first mention of the need for disciples to deny self and take up their cross.

Why Study This Passage on Easter?

We are engaged in a sequential study of the life of Jesus. This passage falls on this Sunday. Later we will have several lessons on the cross and the resurrection as we come to that time in our study of Jesus' life. However, this passage includes several Easter themes: (1) It assures the church of victory over death. (2) It is the first prediction of the death and resurrection by Jesus. (3) This passage helps explain why the disciples later were surprised by both the death and the resurrection of Jesus. (4) It includes the challenge to live by the way of the cross and resurrection.

Word Study: *Christ*

Christos is the Greek equivalent of the Hebrew *messias*. Both words mean "the anointed One." The Old Testament promised a king of David's line who would reign forever. Since kings were anointed, the word *messias* was used to refer to that coming King. Since Christians believe that Jesus is that King, He is called the Christ. Later, the word *Christ* became almost a last name for Jesus.

❖ *Search the Scriptures*

People in general thought of Jesus as a prophet, but Peter confessed Him as the Christ, the Son of the living God. Jesus then promised to build His church on that rock and promised that the gates of Hades would not overcome it. When Jesus began to teach His disciples about the necessity of His death and resurrection, Peter rebuked Jesus, leading Jesus to rebuke Peter. Jesus told them that they too must deny themselves and take up their cross and follow Him.

Jesus' Confirmation of His Identity (Matt. 16:13-17)

Why did Jesus withdraw with His disciples? What was Jesus' favorite title for Himself? Who did the people think Jesus was? What titles did Peter use for Jesus? What does each title mean? Why were the opinions of the people inadequate? What was the source of Peter's insight? These questions are addressed in the comments on these verses.

Verses 13-17: **When Jesus came into the coasts of Caesarea Philippi, he asked his disciples, saying, Whom do men say that I the Son of man am? ¹⁴And they said, Some say that thou art John the Baptist: some, Elias; and** others, Jeremias, or one of the prophets. [15]He saith unto them, But whom say ye that I am? [16]And Simon Peter answered and said, Thou art the Christ, the Son of the living God. [17]And Jesus answered and said unto him, Blessed art thou, Simon Barjona: for flesh and blood hath not revealed it unto thee, but my Father which is in heaven.

The coasts ("region," NIV) of Caesarea Philippi refers to an area about 25 miles northeast of the Sea of Galilee. Few Jews lived in that area. Therefore, Jesus and His disciples could have some time without the pressure of crowds following them. Jesus had been training the disciples, and He wanted to deal with a new revelation of His identity and mission.

Whom do men say that I the Son of man am? Or as we would cast it in today's English, "Who do people say the Son of Man is?" (NIV). Notice that Jesus used His favorite title for Himself, Son of man. Some have thought this title expressed only Jesus' humanity, but it affirms both His deity and His humanity (see Dan. 7:13-14). Jesus used this title because it seldom was used by others as a title for the Messiah. Therefore, Jesus could pour into it the meaning He intended to teach—the Son of man was the One who would suffer, die, and be raised from the dead. He also will come again (vv. 21,27-28).

The disciples told Jesus that some thought He was John the Baptist. John had preached of the nearness of the kingdom, and he had baptized Jesus. After Herod Antipas had executed John, the guilty king heard what Jesus was doing and thought He was John raised from the dead (14:1-2). Jesus described John as the last and greatest of the prophets (11:11-19).

In general, the people thought Jesus was one of the prophets. Some thought He was a specific prophet. Because of the prophecy of Malachi 4:5, some thought He was Elias, the Greek form of the name Elijah. Some identified Him as Jeremias, the Greek form of the name Jeremiah. Perhaps this was because of the strong opposition Jeremiah and Jesus both faced. The people saw Jesus as a prophet. This is an honored term, but it falls short of recognizing who Jesus truly is.

Then Jesus asked them a crucial question: But whom say ye that I am? Simon Peter often spoke first. He said, Thou art the Christ, the Son of the living God. This is the first clear confession of faith by the disciples in Matthew's Gospel. Christ is the Greek word for Messiah. This confession was that Jesus was the promised King of David's line, who would establish an everlasting kingdom. The Son of the living God affirms Jesus as the divine Son of God.

Jesus responded by saying, Blessed art thou, Simon Barjona: for flesh and blood hath not revealed it unto thee, but my Father which is in heaven.

Blessed is *makairos,* the same word used in the Beatitudes. It refers to one on whom the Lord has shown favor. **Barjona** means "son of Jonah" (NIV). **Simon** had not come to this view of Jesus based on human insight. Instead, the **Father** had revealed this to him.

We learn these truths in verses 13-17: (1.) Jesus is the divine-human Son of man-Son of God and the promised Christ (the Messiah). (2.) Anything less than this is inadequate as a title for Jesus. (3.) Our knowledge of who Jesus is comes by divine revelation, not human understanding.

What answers would you give to Jesus if He asked you the question in verse 13? Would you include: a great teacher, a prophet, a good man, only a man? Jesus often is identified with human terms of honor and respect, but He is not identified as the divine Son of God sent to save us. Jesus is a great Teacher, but He is far more. Some people try to speak well of Jesus while refusing to accept Him as Son of God and Savior. Many refer to Him as only a great teacher.

How would you answer the question in verse 15? Your own personal faith is crucial. Do you believe Jesus is who He claimed to be?

Jesus' Intention to Build His Church (Matt. 16:18-20)

What did Jesus mean by **my church**? What is the **rock** on which it is built? What are **the gates of hell** and why will they **not prevail against** the church? What are **the keys of the kingdom of heaven,** and to whom were they given? Why did Jesus command His disciples to **tell no man that he was Jesus the Christ**? How can this be reconciled with the Great Commission (28:18-20)? These questions are addressed by comments on these verses.

Verses 18-20: And I say also unto thee, That thou art Peter, and upon this rock I will build my church; and the gates of hell shall not prevail against it. [19]And I will give unto thee the keys of the kingdom of heaven: and whatsoever thou shalt bind on earth shall be bound in heaven: and whatsoever thou shalt loose on earth shall be loosed in heaven. [20]Then charged he his disciples that they should tell no man that he was Jesus the Christ.

The key words in this passage are **I will build my church.** Church is *ekklesia,* which in Greek usage meant an assembly. The word *ekklesia* is used in the Greek Old Testament to translate the Hebrew *qahal,* which refers to God's people. This is the first use of the word **church** in the Gospels. Only two other uses are found in the Gospels, and all are in Matthew (see also 18:17). Most of the uses of *ekklesia* in the New Testament refer to a local congregation of believers, but a few times the word refers to all God's people. Matthew 16:18 is such a verse.

My is important. The **church** belongs to Jesus Christ, and He is building it. The church is here described as something being built, but this does not mean that it is a building. The church—whether universal or local—is not a literal building. Peter later wrote that the church is a spiritual building made up of people of faith (1 Pet. 2:1-9).

Nearly every word in these verses has been a source of disagreement. For example, what is the **rock** on which Jesus builds His church? Among the main answers are these: Christ Himself (see 1 Cor. 3:11), confession of faith in Christ, the apostolic testimony to Jesus Christ (Eph. 2:20), and Peter alone as the pope. Most non-Roman Catholics accept one or more of the first three. Ephesians 2:20 says that the church is built on the foundation of the apostles, but this refers to their testimony to Jesus, not to them as people.

There are differences of opinion also about **the gates of hell. Hell** translates *hades*. Hades refers to the realm of death, much as does the Hebrew *sheol*. Jesus is pictured as victor over death and the grave (hades). **Prevail** means "overcome" (NIV). "Death itself will not have any power over it" (CEV). This is because it is Christ's church, and Christ overcame death. Revelation 1:18 says that He has "the keys of death and Hades" (NIV). This is one of the Easter emphases in this passage. The church and those who are part of the church will not be defeated by death.

What are **the keys of the kingdom**? Those who believe that Peter alone was given these believe that he and those who succeeded him have the authority to forgive sins. However, only the Lord can forgive sins. The **keys** represent the responsibility of the church to provide opportunities for people to hear and respond to the good news. This is also involved in the power to **bind** and **loose.**

Jesus **charged** ("warned," NIV) the disciples to **tell no man that he was Jesus the Christ.** Later, in the Great Commission, Jesus ordered them to make disciples of all people (Matt. 28:18-20). How can we explain that at one time He told them not to tell and later He told them to tell? During Jesus' ministry, many Jews (including the disciples, see v. 22) were expecting an earthly Messiah who would restore Israel to its former glory under David. Jesus was the Messiah; but as verse 21 shows, He was not their kind of earthly Messiah. Therefore, He did not want to stir up their false hopes.

From verses 18-20 we learn these truths: (1.) The church refers at times to all God's people and at times to a local congregation. (2.) The church belongs to Jesus Christ, whom the church should follow and serve. (3.) Death cannot overcome the church. (4.) The church has the responsibility to open the door of opportunity for others to come to Christ and to enter His church.

Jesus' Prediction of His Death and Resurrection (Matt. 16:21-23)

Why did Jesus say that He must suffer, die, and be raised from the dead? Why did Peter rebuke Jesus? Why did Jesus rebuke Peter? These questions are addressed by comments on these verses.

Verses 21-23: From that time forth began Jesus to show unto his disciples, how that he must go unto Jerusalem, and suffer many things of the elders and chief priests and scribes, and be killed, and be raised again the third day. ²²Then Peter took him, and began to rebuke him, saying, Be it far from thee, Lord: this shall not be unto thee. ²³But he turned, and said unto Peter, Get thee behind me, Satan: thou art an offense unto me: for thou savourest not the things that be of God, but those that be of men.

This was not the first time Jesus had spoken of dying, but it was the first strong statement about the necessity of His death and resurrection. He **began . . . to show** this to His disciples. **Must** is *dei,* which refers to a moral necessity. He did not explain why here, but elsewhere He tied His death and resurrection to salvation from sin and death (20:28). Jesus had to lay down His life to atone for the sins of the world; His resurrection won His victory over death.

He had to **go unto Jerusalem.** In 23:34-39 Jesus spoke of the reputation of Jerusalem for killing the prophets of the Lord. The groups mentioned in verse 21—**elders and chief priests and scribes**—were groups that made up the Sanhedrin, the Jewish high court, which later condemned Jesus and sent Him to Pilate to be crucified. From this point on, Jesus was committed to go to Jerusalem.

Jesus predicted that He **must . . . suffer . . . and be killed, and be raised again.** The death of Jesus for our sins and His resurrection from death are inseparable parts of the gospel of salvation (1 Cor. 15:3-4). The cross without the resurrection would lack power and meaning. The resurrection validated the death of Jesus and provided salvation and new life.

The disciples were surprised and dismayed by both the crucifixion and the resurrection. How could they have felt this way since Jesus so clearly predicted these events? Verse 22 shows why. **Peter took him** ("aside," NIV), **and began to rebuke him. Be it far from thee, Lord** can be translated, "Never, Lord!" (NIV) or "God forbid it, Lord!" (NRSV). Literally, it is "Mercy on you, Lord." **This shall not be unto thee** can be translated, "This shall never happen to you!" (NIV) or "God would never let this happen to you, Lord!" (CEV).

Why did Peter presume to do such a thing? He shared the false notion about an earthly Messiah. In spite of Old Testament prophecies, the Jews of that day could not conceive of the Messiah's suffering and dying. This explains why the followers of Jesus had failed to hear Jesus' prediction of His resurrection. Herschel H. Hobbs commented, "Apparently Peter's mind stopped on the words 'and be killed,' so that he failed to hear 'and be raised again the third day.'"[1]

Jesus' response to Peter was, **Get thee behind me, Satan.** *Hupage* means "get away from." Jesus used the same word when He repulsed Satan's earlier temptations (4:10). **Offense** is *skandalon,* which means "trap" or "stumbling block" (NIV). Peter went from being a "rock" to being a "stumbling block." Jesus accused Peter of thinking like people of the world rather than like a man of God. In other words, Peter was unknowingly an instrument of **Satan** in renewing the temptations of 4:1-11. Those temptations tried to lure Jesus into choosing some way other than the way of the cross.

Here is another Easter emphasis. The resurrection was God's way of demonstrating that the cross was atonement for human sins. The enemies of Jesus thought they had silenced Him, but the resurrection vindicated Him in what He had said about the necessity of His death to atone for human sin.

From verses 21-23 we learned these truths: (1.) After the divine revelation of who He is, Jesus began to show His disciples the necessity of His death and resurrection. (2.) The death and resurrection of Jesus are the heart of the good news. (3.) The disciples were unable to understand at the time, but after the resurrection, they did. (4.) Jesus continued to be tempted to bypass the cross.

Jesus' Call to Self-Denial (Matt. 16:24-28)

What is self-denial? What does it mean to **take up his cross**? Why is what Jesus stated in verse 24 not optional in the life of faith? Why do those who try to **save** their lives end up losing them? Why do those who **lose** their lives for Christ **find** their lives? Why do people often forfeit their souls for some worldly thing? To what time do verses 27 and 28 refer? These questions are addressed in comments on these verses.

Verse 24: **Then said Jesus unto his disciples, If any man will come after me, let him deny himself, and take up his cross, and follow me.**

Peter had reacted at the news that Jesus must suffer, die, and be raised from the dead. Jesus now carried this a step further. He said that anyone who wants to **come after** Him must **deny himself, and take up his cross.** Luke 9:23 says, "take up his cross daily." To put it another way, self-denial and crossbearing are not options in the Christian life. They are not like accessories that we may choose or reject. Too many professed Christians want salvation without such demands as Jesus set forth here. They want a religion without any cost to themselves, a religion of convenience instead of commitment, a religion of comfort without any suffering. It's as if they said, "I'll go where You want me to go, dear Lord—as long as I can keep the comforts to which I am accustomed."

The cross and resurrection are not only the door to the Christian life but also the way of Christian living. We are saved from sin and death by the crucified and risen Lord. We are to live a life of self-giving love like the love Jesus showed on the cross. We find the power to do this in the resurrection power of the Lord. This is what Paul meant by being crucified with Christ (Gal. 2:20) and risen with Him (Rom. 6:3-4,11).

What did Jesus mean by **let him deny himself**? He meant more than denying something for yourself. Following Christ does involve giving up sins, but self-denial means more. It also does not mean that each believer must put himself or herself down as useless. *Self* is a big word today. People put themselves above all things. All kinds of selfish sins are justified by saying something like this: "The purpose of my life is to find fulfillment and happiness on my own terms. After all, I'm worth it." Genuine self-fulfillment and self-esteem are valid, but not the kind that puts the happiness and welfare of self above the will of God and the needs of others. Jesus taught that life ought to be lived in right relationship with God—whom we love supremely—and others—whom we are to love and help. A person who loves God supremely and loves neighbors as oneself will find true fulfillment and joy. This is an underlying meaning of the paradoxes in verses 25-26.

What is meant by **take up his cross**? The Jews were familiar with the Roman practice of executing condemned prisoners by crucifixion. Jesus literally died on a cross, and His followers must be willing to lay down their lives if this is necessary to remain faithful to the Lord. Some of the apostles were put to death, and some of them were literally crucified. Bearing your cross means the same thing as denying self. It is doing in each situation what Jesus did when He laid down His life on the cross. He sacrificed Himself to obey the will of God and to meet the needs of people. Living for God and others is not easy, but the resurrection power and presence of the Spirit of the crucified-risen Lord empowers us to die to self and to live for God and others.

One common misunderstanding is expressed when someone refers to some burden or pain as their "cross to bear." The cross is something we freely choose. It is not some burden or pain that prayer has failed to remove. These things are burdens and thorns in the flesh, but they are not crosses.

Verses 25-26: **For whosoever will save his life shall lose it: and whosoever will lose his life for my sake shall find it. [26]For what is a man profited,**

if he shall gain the whole world, and lose his own soul? or what shall a man give in exchange for his soul?

Verse 25 presents a truth that is also a paradox. The verse contrasts two ways of life. One is the way of seeking fulfillment without regard for the will of God and the needs of others. These people are trying to save their lives by selfish living. Yet those who seek to **save** their lives shall **lose** true life. In their selfish quest for fulfillment and happiness, they will lose the very thing they sought. On the other hand, people who **lose** their lives **for** Christ's **sake shall find** life.

Most people are eagerly trying to grasp for themselves all that they can. They think that the result will be finding the so-called "good life." They are wrong. Their vision proves to be like a mirage in the desert. The more desperately they try to grasp things for themselves, the more they find only sand. Those who follow Christ in the way of the cross and resurrection deny themselves or are willing to lose themselves for Christ and others. These "losers" are the ones who find what the selfish fail to find. They find real life—abundant and eternal. They find self-fulfillment in the best sense of the word. Nothing is so fulfilling as the joy and meaning of doing the will of God and of helping other people.

Another way to state this paradox is in verse 26. People of the world often yield to the temptation to sell themselves cheaply for a little slice of the world. They usually are not aware of having made a bargain with the devil, something for which they will pay dearly. Exchanging your **soul** for anything is the worst mistake anyone can make. Even if we gained **the whole world,** losing our souls leaves us empty and condemned.

Verses 27-28: **For the Son of man shall come in the glory of his Father with his angels; and then he shall reward every man according to his works. [28]Verily I say unto you, There be some standing here, which shall not taste of death, till they see the Son of man coming in his kingdom.**

Jesus stressed two activities of **the Son of man**: laying down His life (see v. 21; Mark 8:31) and coming again. The latter is emphasized in verse 27. The hope of Christ's future coming is another motive for living now according to His will. Christ **shall reward every man** ("each person," NIV) **according to his works.**

Verse 28 is a difficult verse. The wording sounds like Jesus was still referring to the second coming, but Jesus said that what He was describing would happen during the lifetimes of **some standing** there. If Jesus was referring to His second coming, this means that Jesus was mistaken about the time of His coming. The last disciple probably died before the end of the first century. Therefore, Bible-believing Christians believe that the **coming** in verse 28 refers to one or more of the following: the transfiguration, the resurrection, the coming of the Spirit at Pentecost, or the fall of Jerusalem.

From verses 24-28 we have learned these truths: (1.) Not only was it necessary that Jesus go to the cross, but it is necessary that His followers take up the cross. (2.) Self-denial means to relate yourself to God and others. (3.) Bearing a cross can mean laying down your life in dying or in living. (4.) People who seek to look out for themselves will lose their lives, but those who live in right relation to God and others find true life. (5.) Don't forfeit your soul for all or part of the world. (6.) The Son of man will come in the glory of His Father.

❖ *Spiritual Transformations*

Human opinions of the identity of Jesus fall short of the divine revelation of Jesus as the fully human and fully divine Son of man and Son of God. Christ builds His church on a solid foundation over which death has no power, and He gives the church the responsibility to share the good news. Jesus is the Christ, but He also is the Suffering Servant who had to die for our sins and overcome death by His resurrection. Not only was it necessary for Jesus to go the way of the cross and resurrection, but anyone who wants to follow Him must die to self and live the way of the cross by the power of His resurrection.

Base your belief in Jesus on the divine revelation of Him as the fully divine and fully human Son of Man–Son of God. Accept the responsibility and claim the assurance of being in the church. Repent and believe in the crucified and risen Jesus. Deny yourself, take up your cross, and follow Him.

How do you answer the question in verse 15? _____

_____

What does being in Christ's church mean to you? _____

_____

What are the expressions of self-denial in your life? _____

_____

How are the cross and resurrection the way of salvation and the way of life for you? _____

Prayer of Commitment: Lord, help me deny myself, take up my cross daily, and follow You.

[1]Herschel H. Hobbs, *An Exposition of the Gospel of Matthew,* 223.

OBEYING THE LORD OF GLORY

Bible Passage: Matthew 17:1-13
Key Verse: Matthew 17:5

❖ *Significance of the Lesson*

• The *Theme* of this lesson is Jesus' transfiguration.
• The *Life Question* this lesson seeks to address is What does Jesus' lordship mean to me?
• The *Biblical Truth* is that because Jesus is the Lord of glory people should listen to and obey Him.
• The *Life Impact* is to help you obey Jesus.

Obedience and Lordship

Many adults resist the idea of obeying anyone or anything. They feel that obedience is for children; adults make their own determinations. Therefore, they do what they want to do and live however they think they should live.

The biblical worldview assumes that human beings of all ages are subject to hearing and obeying the Word of God. The New Testament reveals Jesus as Lord, whom believers follow and obey. The transfiguration of Jesus was a revelation of His glory, and the voice of the Father told the disciples that Jesus is His Son and that disciples should hear and obey Him.

Understanding the Transfiguration

The context of the transfiguration is the confession of faith by Peter (Matt. 16:13-20); the revelation by Jesus of the necessity of His suffering, death, and resurrection (v. 21); Peter's failure to understand (vv. 22-23); and Jesus' teaching that His followers must live the way of the cross (vv. 24-28). The transfiguration is the next event recorded in the Bible. It was designed to provide further reinforcement of the teachings of Jesus in 16:21,24. The transfiguration in 17:1-13 focuses on the glory of the crucified Lord.

Word Study: *Transfigured*

Transfigured in Matthew 17:2 is *metemorphothe*. The meaning is to "change" or "transform." We get our English word *metamorphosis* from this Greek word. The only examples of the word in the New Testament are in the passive voice. The word is found in Romans 12:2, in which Paul called believers to be "transformed" instead of "conformed." It is also found in 2 Corinthians 3:18 of believers being "changed" by the Lord into His likeness. In Matthew 17:2 it is used of the change in appearance of Jesus when He was transfigured on the mountain.

❖ *Search the Scriptures*

Six days after Peter's confession of Christ at Caesarea Philippi, Jesus took three of His disciples to a mountaintop where He was transfigured before them. Moses and Elijah appeared and talked with Jesus. A voice from heaven repeated what the heavenly voice had said at Jesus' baptism (Matt. 3:17), but this time with the added remark, "Listen to him!" (17:5, NIV). With the cross looming ahead, this brief glimpse of Jesus as the Lord of glory encouraged the disciples to continue following Jesus to Jerusalem. The story of the transfiguration also encourages us to "hear" or "listen to" Jesus and obey Him.

Glorious Lord (Matt. 17:1-4)

Why did Jesus take Peter, James, and John with Him? What appearance did Jesus have when He was transfigured? What is the significance of the appearance of Moses and Elijah? Why did Peter suggest the building of three tabernacles? These questions will be addressed in comments on these verses.

Verses 1-2: And after six days Jesus taketh Peter, James, and John his brother, and bringeth them up into an high mountain apart, ²and was transfigured before them: and his face did shine as the sun, and his raiment was white as the light.

After six days refers to the time since the significant events of 16:13-28. The parallel account in Luke 9:28 has "about . . . eight days." These are only two ways of referring to a week. Matthew (17:1) and Mark (9:2) counted the days between those events; Luke (9:28) counted the days on which the two events took place. The important thing to recognize is that the transfiguration took place soon after Jesus' first revelation of the necessity of His suffering, death, and resurrection. The two are closely linked together.

The purpose of the transfiguration seems to have been to reinforce the truth Jesus had revealed at Caesarea Philippi.

Peter, James, and John his brother are often called "the inner circle" of the twelve disciples. Jesus took these three with Him on several occasions when He did not take the other nine. He took them with Him when He went into the house of Jairus (Mark 5:37) and when He went into the garden of Gethsemane (Matt. 26:37). We are not told why He did this. We do know that **James** was the first of the twelve to be put to death (Acts 12:1-2). **Peter** and **John** were the main leaders of the Jerusalem church in the early period according to Acts 1–12.

Jesus took these three disciples **up into an high mountain apart** ("by themselves," NIV). The Bible does not reveal which mountain this was, but tells us only that is was **an high mountain.** The traditional mount of transfiguration is Mount Tabor in the middle of Galilee, but it is only 1,900 feet above sea level. Some think it was Mount Hermon, which is northeast of Galilee, but at 9,200 feet above sea level it was distant and rugged; and still others think it was Mount Meron, which is northwest of the sea of Galilee and is nearly 4,000 feet above sea level.

Whichever the mountain, Jesus **was transfigured before them.** The meaning of the word *metemorphothe* in this passage is described in verse 2. First, **his face did shine as the sun.** Moses's face had shown when he came down from being with God on Mount Sinai (Ex. 34:29-30). Second, **his raiment was white as the light** ("his clothes became dazzling white," NRSV). This remarkable appearance of the incarnate Son of God testified to His unique relationship with God. The fact that Jesus was transfigured **before them** implies that the purpose was primarily for their benefit. Looking back on this experience, they realized that they had been privileged to see something of the preexistent glory of the Son of God (John 1:1-2,14) and to get a preview of His future glory (2 Pet. 1:16-18).

Luke related that Jesus went up on the mountain to pray, and the transfiguration took place while He was praying (9:28-29). Luke also informed us that the disciples were sleeping (v. 32). Thus the transfiguration possibly took place at night.

Verses 3-4: **And, behold, there appeared unto them Moses and Elias talking with him. [4]Then answered Peter, and said unto Jesus, Lord, it is good for us to be here: if thou wilt, let us make here three tabernacles; one for thee, and one for Moses, and one for Elias.**

The three disciples were no doubt amazed by the appearance of Jesus. Then their amazement must have grown when **there appeared unto them**

Moses and Elias (Elijah). We are not told how the disciples recognized these two Old Testament figures, but somehow their identity was revealed to the three disciples. A more important question is the reason for this unusual appearance of **Moses and Elias** with Jesus as He was transfigured. Verse 3 tells us only that they were **talking with him.** According to Luke 9:31 they talked to Jesus about "his decease which he should accomplish at Jerusalem." "Decease" is *exodos,* which reminds us of both the exodus of Moses and the unusual departure of Elijah. Thus these two came to prepare Jesus for His unique departure from the earth and to emphasize this to the disciples.

Several suggestions have been made about why Moses and Elijah appeared with Jesus. (1) They represented the Law and the Prophets, which Jesus fulfilled. (2) Both Moses and Elijah were associated with the Messianic Age. Malachi 4:5 speaks of Elijah's role. Other Jewish writings of the day associated Moses with the coming of the Messiah. (3) These were two of the three Old Testament men who, according to the Old Testament or Jewish tradition, did not die (Enoch was the other). Moses did die (Deut. 34), but no one ever found his grave. By the first century, some writings said that Moses was taken by the Lord without dying. (4) Moses and Elijah both had unusual departures. (5) Since the transfiguration came immediately after the revelation by Jesus of His suffering, death, and resurrection, Moses and Elijah came to affirm Jesus in this commitment and to reemphasize for the disciples what Jesus had told the disciples in Matthew 16:21. This view is supported by Jesus' repetition of this in 17:12. Jesus continued to tell the disciples of His coming death and resurrection. In fact, He did so after they went down the mountain (see vv. 22-23).

Peter was one of those people who enter into every situation with an open mouth. He occasionally said something true and important. At other times, Peter's words were wrong or out of place. This seems to be the case here. Mark 9:6 and Luke 9:33 state that Peter didn't know what he was saying. **Lord, it is good for us to be here** was surely true, but his suggestion about building **three tabernacles** ("shelters," NIV; "dwellings," NRSV) missed the point of the transfiguration. The Jews built temporary booths for the Feast of Tabernacles. Peter wanted to build **one for** Jesus, **one for Moses,** and **one for Elias.** We are not told why Peter made this suggestion. Perhaps he thought it would be a way to honor the Lord and these two great men of the past. Perhaps he wanted to prolong this special time on the mountain. Some Bible students think that this was a way of offering an alternative for the cross to Jesus. "Peter's implication was still in line with his rebuke of Jesus a few days before. Why descend to the plain and resume the conflict? Why go to Jerusalem and die? Would it not be better to remain on the mount in this heavenly fellowship?"[1]

The voice from heaven brought the three disciples back to God's intention for the transfiguration. The transfiguration was a preview of the coming glory of the Lord after His resurrection from the dead. The transfiguration of Jesus was a revelation of the lordship of Jesus Christ—a lordship fully revealed only after He suffered and died.

Preeminent Son (Matt. 17:5-8)

How is verse 5 similar to and different from Matthew 3:17? What is the significance of **hear ye him**? How did the disciples respond to the voice from heaven? How did Jesus help them? These questions will be addressed in comments on verses 5-8.

Verse 5: **While he yet spake, behold, a bright cloud overshadowed them: and behold a voice out of the cloud, which said, This is my beloved Son, in whom I am well pleased; hear ye him.**

The **bright cloud** is reminiscent of the cloud that the Israelites saw over Mount Sinai when the Lord made a covenant with them and they heard "the voice of the trumpet exceeding loud" (Ex. 19:16). A cloud also **over-shadowed** the newly built tabernacle. This cloud showed that "the glory of the LORD filled the tabernacle" (40:34). The Lord led the people with a cloud by day and a pillar of fire by night (vv. 36-38). This cloud signified the glory of the Lord's presence.

If there was any doubt of this, **a voice out of the cloud** spoke, saying, **This is my beloved Son, in whom I am well pleased.** These are the same words spoken by God when Jesus was baptized, except that God on that occasion spoke primarily to Jesus. The words reflect two Old Testament passages. **My beloved Son** reflects the Old Testament prophecies of the Messiah-Son of God (Ps. 2:7). **In whom I am well pleased** comes from one of the Servant passages (Isa. 42:1). Together they combine two strands of Old Testament prophecy concerning Jesus. He was the Messiah-King; and He would fulfill His mission through suffering, death, and resurrection. In other words, verse 5 reinforced the words of Jesus in Matthew 16:21, which Peter and the others were resisting.

God spoke these words on the mount of transfiguration for the benefit of the disciples. The transfiguration was done "before them" (v. 2). God was giving them a revelation designed to reinforce what Jesus was trying to teach them. This view is supported by what God said to the disciples, **Hear ye him.**

The word **hear** in the Bible assumes that the one who hears God's voice or words will obey what He says. There are several stages involved in hearing and obeying. Those who hear must give their full attention to what is said: "Who hath ears to hear, let him hear" (13:9). They must understand what they hear (vv. 14,19,23). And they must act on what they hear (7:24-27).

A missionary translator was struggling to find a word for *obedience*, but couldn't. One day he called his dog to him, and the dog came running. A national said, "Your dog was all ear." This gave the translator the word he needed for *obedience*—"to be all ear."[2]

How are Christians today to hear what the Lord Jesus is telling us to do? He speaks to us through the Holy Scriptures. We are to obey the clear commands of the Lord in the Bible. In seeking His will in personal leadership, we must stay in touch with Him through prayer and follow the leadership of His Spirit. This passage gives a clear example of something Jesus says to every believer—it is stated in Matthew 16:24.

Verses 6-8: *And when the disciples heard it, they fell on their face, and were sore afraid.* [7]*And Jesus came and touched them, and said, Arise, and be not afraid.* [8]*And when they had lifted up their eyes, they saw no man, save Jesus only.*

Hearing this voice caused the three **disciples** to fall **on their face** because they **were sore afraid** ("terrified," NIV). **Jesus came and touched them,** a touch accompanied by His words, **Arise, and be not afraid.** Peter especially must have felt uncomfortable. He had been the one who rebuked the Lord when Jesus first predicted His suffering, death, and resurrection. He was also the one who spoke out of turn on the mount of transfiguration. Notice that Jesus not only spoke to them but also **touched them.** His touch was as much a sign of acceptance as His words.

The three were on their faces. **When they had lifted up their eyes, they saw no man, save Jesus only.** This probably means not only that Moses and Elijah had departed, but that Jesus Himself was no longer glowing. Now they were expected to apply what they had heard and experienced to everyday life. And they were expected to listen to and obey Jesus.

What had they learned? Ideally they had learned that Jesus was going to suffer, die, and rise again by the will of God. Later passages show that they had not yet learned this lesson completely. They continued not to understand the necessity of the cross and the resurrection (Mark 9:31-32). They also were supposed to have learned to obey the word of God—whether spoken from heaven by God or spoken on earth by His Son.

The transfiguration included several marvels: the changed appearance of Jesus, the appearance of Moses and Elijah, and the voice from heaven. These were revelations of God, which showed that the cross and the resurrection were God's plan. The glory of God was revealed by these revelations. They foreshadowed the coming glory of the resurrection of Jesus and of His future coming. However, the way to the crown involved a cross for Jesus, and it also does for us.

If we would obey the Lord, the place to begin is in this clear call to follow Him in the way of the cross. But as Blomberg pointed out, "The message that suffering must precede glory remains scandalous even today for many people, including professing Christians."[3]

Christians who are persecuted understand what Jesus meant. The International Mission Board reported the following story from China. The pastor of an underground church was talking about security to a group of Southern Baptist visitors. Every time his church reached 10 to 15 members it split, he said. Too many members would attracted attention from the government. For the same reason, each church constantly changed meeting locations. To find out where the church was meeting that day, church members visited an usher on a downtown street, who would tell them. One usher, whom the government identified, was arrested, beaten, and put in prison. He lost his job, his medical benefits, and his house. Another believer then stepped forward to take the usher's place, but he too was found out, beaten, and put in prison. One visitor said to the pastor, "I suppose you have difficulty filling that job." "No," the pastor responded, "we have a waiting list."

Suffering Savior (Matt. 17:9-13)

Why did Jesus command the three disciples to tell no one what had happened until after the resurrection? What did the **scribes** believe about Elijah's coming? What did Jesus teach on this subject? How did Jesus say that the experience of John the Baptist would also be His experience? These questions are addressed in the comments on these verses.

Verse 9: **And as they came down from the mountain, Jesus charged them, saying, Tell the vision to no man, until the Son of man be risen again from the dead.**

The Lord had given to these three disciples a mountaintop experience of divine revelation and glory. But now they headed **down from the mountain** to the valley below. Jesus told them to **tell the vision** ("what you have seen," NIV) **to no man.** This is the last of these prohibitions in Matthew (see 8:4;

9:30; 12:16; 16:20). Most of the people were looking for an earthly Messiah, but one filled with divine glory. Jesus had come to suffer, die, and be raised from the dead. Mark 9:10 shows that the disciples still did not understand what Jesus meant by the resurrection from the dead, even after this experience.

This restriction would be lifted after **the Son of man** was **risen again from the dead.** After His resurrection, the disciples were to tell everyone about Him, because only then would their own ideas of the Messiah include the cross and resurrection. When we read the preaching of Peter and Paul in the Book of Acts, we find them stressing the atoning death of Jesus for sinners and His resurrection from the dead, which showed that He is alive and the Victor over sin and its ally death.

Verses 10-13: **And his disciples asked him, saying, Why then say the scribes that Elias must first come?** [11]**And Jesus answered and said unto them, Elias truly shall first come, and restore all things.** [12]**But I say unto you, That Elias is come already, and they knew him not, but have done unto him whatsoever they listed. Likewise shall also the Son of man suffer of them.** [13]**Then the disciples understood that he spake unto them of John the Baptist.**

The appearance of Elijah at the transfiguration caused the disciples to wonder about the differences of opinion on the fulfillment of Malachi 4:5-6. **The scribes** believed **that Elias** would come **first.** They also believed that he would **restore all things.** The disciples asked Jesus about this. Jesus clarified the matter by stating that **Elias truly shall first come, and restore all things** ("To be sure, Elijah comes and will restore all things," NIV). In Greek, **come** is present tense, and **restore** is future tense. Jesus was reflecting the way **the scribes** spoke of it. Jesus corrected this view by pointing out several things: (1) **Elias is come already** ("Elijah has already come," NIV). Verse 13 shows that the disciples correctly **understood** that Jesus was speaking of **John the Baptist.** Although John had denied being Elijah literally (John 1:21), Jesus identified John as the fulfillment of Malachi 4:5-6 (see Matt. 11:10-14). (2) The people to whom he came **knew him not.** "They did not recognize" (NIV) who he was. (3) They **have done unto him whatsoever they listed** ("everything they wished," NIV). In other words, they rejected him and he was killed. (4) The rejection and death of John the Baptist foreshadowed the way Jesus would be treated—**Likewise shall also the Son of man suffer.**

Jesus thus brought the conversation back to the central message for the disciples. Jesus was to suffer, die, and be raised from the dead. He repeated this in verses 22-23. Verse 23 states that the disciples "were exceeding sorry." But Mark 9:32 says that "they understood not that saying, and were afraid to ask him."

❖ *Spiritual Transformations*

When the transfiguration pointed to the coming death of Jesus, Peter showed a continuing failure to understand. The transfiguration reemphasized Jesus' prediction of His suffering, death, and resurrection, and called the disciples to hear, understand, and obey. As Jesus and the three disciples came down the mountain, Jesus continued to point to His death and resurrection. The transfiguration was designed to show Jesus' disciples that He is the glorious Lord, the preeminent Son, and the Suffering Savior. The transfiguration calls us to confess Jesus' lordship and listen to and obey the Lord of glory.

Thus "Hear ye him" are the key words as we apply this lesson to our lives. Hearing in the biblical sense involves: (1) being where you can hear what the Lord says, (2) paying attention to what He says, (3) getting rid of your own preconceptions and accepting what He says, (4) understanding what He says, and (5) obeying any command He gives.

In this passage (as in Matt. 16:13-28 last week), the revelation was that Jesus must suffer, die, and be raised from the dead. The command was to hear or obey Him, as last week it was to take up our cross and follow Him. The disciples were having trouble really hearing this because it did not fit what they had expected the Messiah to do and what they expected Him to tell them to do. What about you?

Is there anything that hinders you from hearing or obeying Jesus? _____

_____

Check each of the following things you do in order to obey Him:
___ *Seek every opportunity to read or hear His Word.*
___ *Set aside preconceptions and let the Lord speak to me.*
___ *Obey each of the Lord's commands and follow where He leads.*

"Take up your cross," the Savior said, "If you would My disciple be;
  Deny yourself, the world forsake, And humbly follow after Me."
Take up your cross and follow Christ; Think not till death to lay it down;
  For only those who bear the cross May hope to wear the glorious crown.[4]

Prayer of Commitment: Lord, help me to hear, understand, and obey Your Word.

[1]J. W. Shephard, *The Christ of the Gospels* [Grand Rapids: William B. Eerdmans Publishing Company, 1954], 316.
[2]Zuck, *The Speaker's Quote Book,* 268.
[3]Blomberg, "Matthew," NAC, 262.
[4]Charles W. Everest, "Take Up Your Cross," No. 494, *The Baptist Hymnal,* 1991.

Week of April 29

BEING A NEIGHBOR

Bible Passage: Luke 10:25-37
Key Verse: Luke 10:33

❖ *Significance of the Lesson*

• The *Theme* of this lesson is that Jesus confronts personal prejudices.
• The *Life Question* this lesson seeks to address is Why do I have difficulty loving some people?
• The *Biblical Truth* is that loving one's neighbor transcends all boundaries, including those of race, nationality, region, and class.
• The *Life Impact* is to help you demonstrate love toward all people.

Adults and the Command to Love Neighbors

Adults who hold secular worldviews narrowly define neighbors as people like themselves. Many adults have a small circle of people whom they love and help. Prejudice causes some adults to exclude from their circle people of different races, nationalities, regions, or social status.

In the biblical worldview, loving one's neighbor transcends all boundaries, including those of race, nationality, region, and social status. Such love is demonstrated by acting for the good of others.

The Parables in Luke

Many of the most familiar parables of Jesus are recorded only in Luke. In addition to the parable of the good Samaritan, which is the biblical text for this lesson, Luke recorded the following parables: the rich fool, the lost sheep, the lost coin, the prodigal son, the dishonest steward, the friend at midnight, the unjust judge, the Pharisee and the publican, the pounds, and the rich man and Lazarus (if this last one is to be considered a parable).

Three Approaches to the Parable of the Good Samaritan

1. Some interpret it as an allegory. They make each person or thing have some hidden meaning. The traveler represents Adam or lost humanity

(going away from the holy city). The thieves represent the devil. The priest is the Law and the Levite is the Prophets. The Samaritan is Jesus. The inn is the church. The two pence are the Old and New Testaments. There is no evidence to support such an interpretation. Allegorical interpretations enable each person to make anything mean anything they choose.

2. Some people see it as a simple story with a lesson that anyone can live by. That is, it teaches people to be humanitarians. These people do not connect the parable to the need for salvation and God's help to practice this kind of love.

3. Most Christians see the parable not as teaching salvation by good works but as the kind of costly, self-giving love that can only be practiced through the grace and power of the Spirit of the crucified and risen Lord.

Word Study: *Neighbor*

The Greek word translated **neighbor** in verses 27,29,36 is *plesios,* which literally means "near by" or "close by." It is used here as a substantive meaning "the one who is near." This is a different word for "neighbors" than *perioikoi,* which means "living around." The latter word appears in 1:58 to describe the neighbors who came to see the newborn baby of Zechariah and Elizabeth. Jesus defined a *plesios* as a fellow human being.

❖ *Search the Scriptures*

When an expert in the Jewish Law asked Jesus what he should do to inherit eternal life, Jesus asked him what the Law said. When the lawyer answered by quoting Deuteronomy 6:5 and Leviticus 19:18, Jesus told him he had answered right and that he would live if he did these things. In an attempt to justify himself, the man asked Jesus, "Who is my neighbor?" Jesus told a story of a man who was robbed, beaten, and left dying along the road from Jerusalem to Jericho. A priest and then a Levite saw the injured man and passed by on the other side, but a Samaritan stopped and did all he could to help the injured man. When Jesus asked the lawyer which one acted as a neighbor, the lawyer said the one who showed mercy. Jesus told him to go and do likewise.

Important Questions (Luke 10:25-29)

In what way was the lawyer trying to test Jesus by his question? Did Jesus' responses teach salvation by keeping the Law? In what way did the lawyer hope to justify himself by his second question? What did the lawyer reveal about himself by his second question? These questions are addressed in comments on verses 25-29?

Verses 25-29: **And, behold, a certain lawyer stood up, and tempted him, saying, Master, what shall I do to inherit eternal life?** [26]**He said unto him, What is written in the law? how readest thou?** [27]**And he answering said, Thou shalt love the Lord thy God with all thy heart, and with all thy soul, and with all thy strength, and with all thy mind; and thy neighbor as thyself.** [28]**And he said unto him, Thou hast answered right; this do, and thou shalt live.** [29]**But he, willing to justify himself, said unto Jesus, And who is my neighbor?**

A **lawyer** (*nomikos*) was an expert in the law. A Jewish **lawyer** was an expert in the Old Testament Law. He **stood up** apparently from a session in which Jesus was teaching. Luke told us that he **tempted** Jesus. The word is *ekpeirazon,* an even stronger word than the more usual *peirazo.* The word can mean either "to tempt" or "to test" (NIV, HCSB). In other words, at least part of his reason for asking the question was to test Jesus in some way. Some Bible students think that he was only testing Jesus' ability as a teacher. Others think he had a more hostile purpose. He may have hoped to be able to show his knowledge of the Law to be superior to that of Jesus. He may have even hoped to trap Jesus into saying something that could be used against Him.

His question in verse 25 is worded similarly to the question of the rich young ruler (18:18). **Eternal life** here means the same thing as being saved or entering the kingdom. This is an important question because **eternal life** is the deepest human need. Some Bible students believe that the man's question reveals that he thought that **eternal life** could be attained by his own righteousness. If so, he probably wanted to ensure that he had done all he could to **inherit eternal life.** One of the key words in the passage is *poieo,* which means to **do** or "practice." The lawyer used it in verse 25, and Jesus used it in verses 28 and 37.

Whatever the lawyer meant, Jesus did not mean that salvation is by doing good on our own. Jesus began where the man was. The man was an expert in the Law; therefore, Jesus asked him what the Law said on the subject. In a sense, Jesus turned the tables on the lawyer. The man tested Jesus with his question. Jesus answered with a question that tested the lawyer—**What is written in the law? how readest thou?**

The lawyer quoted Deuteronomy 6:5 and Leviticus 19:18. Jesus Himself quoted the same two verses when asked about the greatest commandment (Matt. 22:37-39; Mark 12:30-31). In this passage, it was the lawyer who used these two verses to sum up the Old Testament answer to his own question. How did he have the insight to give this answer to his own question? Some

Jewish teachers had brought together these two verses. The man may have known about this, or he may have heard Jesus teach it. Jesus brought these two commandments together several times in His ministry (again, see Matt. 22:37-39; Mark 12:30-31). The command for wholehearted love for God covers the first four of the Ten Commandments, and the command to love our neighbor covers the last six of the Commandments. The question about loving neighbors is the one on which this passage concentrates.

Jesus told the lawyer that he had answered **right** ("correctly," NIV, HCSB). He added, **This do, and thou shalt live.** Jesus was not teaching salvation by good works here. He was responding to the lawyer's question in the same context as the lawyer's answer to His question. The Law taught that those who live by it would live (Lev. 18:5). That is, anyone who loves God totally is in right relationship with God. Loving God totally is another way for describing saving faith.

Perhaps the lawyer should have accepted Jesus' commendation and not asked the next question. However, we can be grateful he did, because it led Jesus to tell the parable of the good Samaritan. The man asked his second question because he wanted **to justify himself. Justify** is *dikaiosai*, which means "to justify" or "to vindicate" (NEB). The word is used most often for being counted righteous by God, but it also at times refers to being vindicated or justified in the sight of others (see 16:15). The lawyer seems to have felt that he had looked foolish by asking and answering his own question. Therefore, "the man wanted to show that he knew what he was talking about" (CEV), so he asked another question. We are not told whether this was a sincere question or whether he was still trying to test Jesus.

Unfortunately for him, his second question—**and who is my neighbor?**—revealed more about him than he intended to reveal. This question showed that the man had a limited group whom he considered neighbors. It also implied that he was anxious to exclude some people from this circle of responsibility to love. Typically, the Jews of that day restricted neighbors to their own people. They certainly did not consider Gentiles or Samaritans as neighbors. Jesus' parable addressed the second question of the lawyer, not the first.

Before we cast any stones at the lawyer, we must ask ourselves if we too do not restrict the list of people whom we are to love. Sometimes we exclude large groups of people because they are not our kind of people. Because of modern technology and mobility our world has shrunk. A first-century person met only a limited number and kinds of people. In our world the news media make us aware instantly of problems on the other side of the earth. People of all races, nationalities, and social classes are present in the

United States. Demagogues use their presence to stir up the worst aspects of human nature by words of scorn toward those who are different.

We are reluctant to broaden the scope of our definition of **neighbor** for another reason. We do not have the resources to meet the infinite needs of all the people in the world, in our land, or even in our neighborhoods. Thus we try to trim down the list to what we can manage. The Lord does not expect any one of His children to meet all the needs of humanity; He does expect us to see the world as a neighborhood and to do what we can to help those who cross our path. The lawyer's questions were important questions indeed.

Callous Indifference (Luke 10:30-32)

Was Jesus' story based on an actual event? How could the thieves be so callous? Why did the priest and Levite pass by the injured man? How might they have justified themselves? How serious was their sin?

Verses 30-32: **And Jesus answering said, A certain man went down from Jerusalem to Jericho, and fell among thieves, which stripped him of his raiment, and wounded him, and departed, leaving him half dead.** [31]**And by chance there came down a certain priest that way: and when he saw him, he passed by on the other side.** [32]**And likewise a Levite, when he was at the place, came and looked on him, and passed by on the other side.**

Not all of Jesus' parables have the word *parable* attached to them. Most people consider Luke 10:30-35 to be a parable. We do not know if this was an actual event, but we do know that the setting was realistic. The road that **went down from Jerusalem to Jericho** was a dangerous road, and **thieves** often attacked travelers, especially if the traveler was alone. Since it was the most direct route from Jerusalem to Jericho, the road often was used by merchants and other travelers.

We do not know much about the **certain man** in the story. We are not told his race or nationality. We are not told why he was making this dangerous trip alone. All we know is that he was a **man.** He was a fellow human being to all the others in the story. Thus Jesus used him as a symbol of every person. In Shakespeare's play "The Merchant of Venice" is a poignant plea by Shylock, a Jew, to be considered as a fellow human being by the others in the story. Shakespeare has him asking: "Hath not a Jew eyes? hath not a Jew hands, organs, dimensions, senses, affections, passions? . . . If you prick us, do we not bleed? if you tickle us, do we not laugh? if you poison us, do we not die?"[1]

The man in Jesus' story **fell among thieves. Fell among** is *periepesan,* which means to "fall into the hands of." Notice the words that describe how the robbers treated the hapless traveler: They **stripped him of his raiment, and wounded him, and departed, leaving him half dead.** Being thieves, they surely took whatever of value he had. Perhaps he did not have as much as they expected and in their anger they stripped off his clothes, beat him, and left him to die. This kind of brutality may have been their usual practice for all victims. In every society are people like these bandits. They prey upon others, seemingly without any sense of humanity, concern, or conscience. We wonder how such people live with themselves, but they seem untroubled by their brutality. They are the brutal predators of the world. Some of them use outward violence. Others hurt people in different ways. Jeremiah accused the people of his day of making the temple into a den of thieves by their callous cruelty toward the needy (Jer. 7:9-11). Jesus applied the same passage to the high priests who used the temple to exploit people (Luke 19:45-46). Others who preyed on people included dishonest merchants (Amos 8:4-6), employers who withheld wages from workers (Jas. 5:1-5), and greedy people who used their power to get what they wanted (1 Kings 21).

Then Jesus said, **By chance there came down a certain priest.** When the lawyer heard this line of the story, he probably expected the priest to have been led that way by divine providence. Help seemed on the way when this man of God **saw** the dying victim. The lawyer and other Jews who were listening no doubt expected this holy man to stop and help the victim. Instead Jesus said, **he passed by on the other side.**

Next came by **a Levite.** A **Levite** was a member of the tribe of Levi but not of Aaron's priestly family. The Levites were responsible for certain tasks at the temple and functioned as priests' assistants. Three terms indicate that his action was similar to the priest's action: the use of the word **likewise** (*homoios*), the reuse of the words translated **and when he saw him** (*kai idon*; which are rendered **and looked on him** in the KJV in v. 32), and the reuse of the word translated **passed by on the other side** (*antiparelthen*). Some manuscript copies of Luke have the additional word *genomenos*, "having happened by." "The possible addition of *genomenos* (happened by) with *elthon* (coming) suggests that he took a closer look (*idon*, seeing) at the man and the place where he lay, and then he walked away. If so, then the disappointment with the lack of help is heightened."[2]

Jesus did not give any insight into why these two men, who represented religious people, acted this way. Many have speculated that a priest might use the law that forbade touching a dead body. Others have pointed out that they may have feared that the thieves were hiding near-by, using the wounded man as bait for someone else. For whatever reason, both **passed by on the other side.**

Here are three kinds of people. The **thieves** were predators who preyed on the helpless. The **man** was a victim of the callous greed of others and the neglect of good people who did nothing. The **priest** and **Levite** were religious people who failed to help a fellow human being in need. How serious were the sins of the thieves? They robbed, beat, stripped, and left a man to die. The other two also left a man to die. They did not put him in the ditch to die, but they saw him there and did nothing to help. This was a sin of omission, and a serious one. Theirs was the sin of callous indifference.

The Bible gives many examples of people who pass by on the other side. These include rich people who ignore the poor at their gates (16:19-31), church people who claim to have faith but who fail to help the needy (Jas. 2:14-17), and those who do nothing to help the needy (Matt. 25:44-45).

Compassionate Action (Luke 10:33-35)

What surprises did Jesus' story contain? What did the Samaritan do to help the injured man? What does this reveal about *agape* love? These questions are addressed in comments on verses 33-35.

Verses 33-35: **But a certain Samaritan, as he journeyed, came where he was: and when he saw him, he had compassion on him, [34]and went to him, and bound up his wounds, pouring in oil and wine, and set him on his own beast, and brought him to an inn, and took care of him. [35]And on the morrow when he departed, he took out two pence, and gave them to the host, and said unto him, Take care of him; and whatsoever thou spendest more, when I come again, I will repay thee.**

Jesus' parables were realistic to life, but He often added surprises for His hearers. This story had at least two surprises for the lawyer and others who first heard the story. The first surprise was the failure of the priest and Levite to help the man. The second surprise was that a **Samaritan** did what the others had failed to do. The first word in verse 33 in the Greek is *Samarites* (**Samaritan**). The Jews and the Samaritans held each other in contempt. The two religious Jews had passed by the injured man, but who stopped to help him? The lawyer must have been shocked when Jesus made a Samaritan the hero of the story.

Keep in mind that Jesus was answering the question, **Who is my neighbor?** Jews and Samaritans did not think of one another as neighbors; they more often considered each other enemies. Luke 9:51-56 illustrates this. A village in Samaria refused to allow Jesus and the disciples to pass through, and some of Jesus' disciples wanted to call down fire from heaven on them. By His own example, Jesus showed that He did not share this prejudice (see also John 4:1-42; Acts 1:8). Thus Jesus was broadening the definition of *neighbor* for both groups. Anyone in need is a neighbor.

The Samaritan's actions help with another key word in Leviticus 19:18— "love." We usually think of *love* as primarily a feeling or emotion. Emotion may be involved, but Christian love, *agapeseis* (v. 27), is primarily an action. Notice how Jesus described the Samaritan and what he did. The word **saw** and **looked** are the same word (*idon*) of all three who saw the man. The Samaritan **saw** him through eyes of love and concern. Thus **he had compassion on him. Had compassion** is *esplanchnisthe* (from *splanchnizomai*), the same word often used to describe the compassion of Jesus (see Matt. 9:36). The Samaritan's compassion, like that of Jesus, was seen in his actions on behalf of someone. We do not know what else the Samaritan felt. He may have felt fear that the thieves were lurking nearby. He may have felt revulsion at the bloody, naked body in the ditch. Jesus emphasized what the Samaritan did more than what he felt.

Notice all the words that describe the many actions of the Samaritan. The Samaritan **went to him, and bound up** ("bandaged," NIV, HCSB) **his wounds, pouring in oil and wine.** Both **oil** and **wine** were used for such injuries. Then he **set him on his own beast** ("donkey," NIV), **and brought him to an inn, and took care of him.** When he left the next day, the Samaritan gave money to the innkeeper and told him to use the money to care for the injured man. The **two pence** literally is "two denarii" (NKJV, NASB, NRSV, HCSB). A denarius was a small silver coin equal to a day's wages (see Matt. 20:2,9,13). Hence the *New International Version's* and the *Contemporary English Version's* rendering of "two silver coins" (see also the NEB's and REB's "two silver pieces"). The Samaritan also told the innkeeper that if the victim's care cost even more, he would **repay** the innkeeper when he returned. These are an impressive list of actions on the Samaritan's part.

Genuine Christian love involves doing good for others. It is costly and risky. This foreigner risked his own life, gave the dying man first aid, used his own animal to carry the man (which meant that he probably had to walk or dispose of whatever the animal was carrying). He gave time, energy, and money to ensure that the injured man would receive adequate care. One reason Christians often do not act as good Samaritans is that we know helping another person often is risky and always is costly. Therefore, we sometimes follow the priest and the Levite in passing by on the other side and going on our way.

The Samaritan had a different philosophy of life from the thieves and from the priest and Levite. Many have summarized these three philosophies like this: The thieves said, "What's thine is mine; I'll take it." The priest and the

Levite said, "What's mine is mine; I'll keep it." The Samaritan said, "What's mine is thine; I'll give it."

A 12-year old boy was baby-sitting his younger brother. The older boy was outside when someone cried that their house was on fire. He knew that his little brother was trapped inside and unable to save himself. The older brother ran into the burning house, found his little brother, and carried him to safety. The people of his neighborhood told him he was very brave to do this. They asked him, "What were you thinking when you rushed into the burning house?" The boy said, "I wasn't thinking about anything. *I just heard my brother's cry.*"

Jesus taught us to love not only our brothers but our neighbors, and even our enemies. Love means acting for their good whatever the risk or cost to us.

Divine Command (Luke 10:36-37)

Why did the lawyer never say the word *Samaritan*? How did the story answer the lawyer's second question?

Verses 36-37: Which now of these three, thinkest thou, was neighbor unto him that fell among the thieves? [37]**And he said, He that showed mercy on him. Then said Jesus unto him, Go, and do thou likewise.**

Jesus asked the lawyer, **Which now of these three** acted like a **neighbor** to the injured man? Notice how Jesus had modified the lawyer's question in verse 29. The lawyer had asked, "Who is my neighbor?" Jesus asked him to identify which of the three was a neighbor to the injured man. The lawyer asked the wrong question. The real question is, "To whom can I be a neighbor?" or "What can I do to help my neighbor?"

The lawyer answered, **He that showed mercy on him** acted as a neighbor. Notice that the lawyer could not bring himself to say "the Samaritan." This word must have stuck in his throat. Prejudice is a prime factor in defining who people consider as neighbors. Judging people is bad, but prejudging them on the basis of some human characteristic is worse. Whole groups of people automatically are excluded from the status of neighbors whom we should help. Peter had to learn this lesson when the Lord led him to the household of Cornelius (Acts 10:1–11:25). James, Jesus' earthly brother, rebuked church people who honored a wealthy visitor and neglected a poor one (Jas. 2:1-8).

Go, and do thou likewise is another example of the word **do** (*poiei*). The emphasis is on doing, acting, practicing.

There are three main components in the command, "Thou shalt love thy neighbor as thyself" (Lev. 19:18; Luke 10:27). One is the scope of the word **neighbor.** The parable teaches that all people are our neighbors. The second question is the meaning of **love.** The parable shows that Christian *agape* is acting for the good of others. The third component is the meaning of **as thyself.** These words have been interpreted in several ways. Some think that Jesus meant that rather than the self-love of a sinful, selfish life, we are to love our neighbor instead. Others think He meant that we are to build on the love we have for ourselves and love our neighbor as we love ourselves. Still others emphasize that our love for ourselves and for others is rooted in God's love for all people. Thus they begin with this love of God as the foundation and motivation for loving others and having a proper regard for ourselves.

❖ *Spiritual Transformations*

This parable has many applications for followers of Jesus: All people are our neighbors, especially those in need of the help we can provide. Christian love means doing good for others, regardless of how we feel. God's love for all people is the foundation for loving others and having proper regard for ourselves.

Edgar Watson Howe wrote: "I do not love my neighbor as myself, and apologize to no one. I treat my neighbor as fairly and politely as I hope to be treated, but there is no law in nature or common sense ordering me to go beyond that."[3] *How do you respond to what he wrote?* _____

Which person do you most identify yourself with in the story? Why? _____

_____

Why is it religious people seldom want to identify themselves with the religious people in this story? Does this give you any clues how those who are hurting and in need of help see religious persons? _____

Every place has people in these four categories: victims, predators who prey on others, people who do nothing to help the victims, and people who do what they can to help victims. *What kinds of people are in each category in the area where you live?* _____

If Jesus were telling this story today in your part of the country, from what group would He make the good Samaritan? _____

Prayer of Commitment: Lord, help me to recognize my neighbors and to love them as You love them and me.

[1]William Shakespeare, "The Merchant of Venice," Act III, Scene I, in *The Works of William Shakespeare* [New York: Oxford University Press, 1904], 401.

[2]Darrell L. Bock, *Luke 9:51–24:53,* in Baker Exegetical Commentary on the New Testament [Grand Rapids: Baker Books, 1996], 1031.

[3]Edgar Watson Howe, in *Success Easier Than Failure* (1917), as cited in *American Quotations,* edited by Gorton Carruth and Eugene Ehrlich [New York: Wing Books, 1988], 148.

TALKING WITH GOD

Bible Passage: Luke 11:1-13
Key Verse: Luke 11:9

❖ *Significance of the Lesson*

• The *Theme* of this lesson is Jesus taught His followers how to pray.
• The *Life Question* this lesson seeks to address is How should I pray?
• The *Biblical Truth* is that believers consistently can pray with confidence that God hears and graciously answers their prayers.
• The *Life Impact* is to help you pray consistently.

Does God Answer Prayer?

The secular worldview discourages a life of prayer. Many do not believe that God exists. They consider prayer to be an exercise in futility, a self-delusion, a psychological crutch. Many people claim to have prayed at some time in their lives, but they often think of prayer only as asking for something. Such people fall back on prayer when all else fails.

The biblical worldview teaches that God knows and cares for people. Those who have a faith relationship with Him are encouraged to pray with praise, thanksgiving, petition, confession, and intercession. Prayer changes things and it changes the one who prays.

Luke's Emphasis on Prayer

Prayer is taught throughout the Bible, but the emphasis on prayer in Luke is especially strong. The terms *prayer* and *pray* are found 13 times in Mark and 17 times in Matthew. But they are found 21 times in Luke and 25 times in Acts. Luke begins with prayer (1:9-10). The prayer life of Jesus is emphasized. He prayed at His baptism (3:21), before He selected the twelve (6:12), before He asked the disciples who He was (9:18), when He was transfigured (vv. 28-29), for Peter (22:32), in Gethsemane (v. 42). Three sayings of Jesus from the cross are recorded in Luke: two of the three are prayers (23:34,46).

The Model Prayer in Matthew 6:9-13 and in Luke 11:2-4

The Lord's Prayer or the Model Prayer is recorded in both Matthew 6:9-13 and in Luke 11:2-4. Some of the oldest copies of Luke's Gospel contain a shorter version than Matthew recorded in his Gospel. The *New International Version* follows the shorter ancient manuscripts, while the *King James Version* is based on later copies of Luke and contains a longer version that is more like that found in Matthew's Gospel. The *Holman Christian Standard Bible* agrees with the *New International Version* and adopts the shorter version of Jesus' prayer in Luke 11:2-4.

Some Bible students think that Jesus taught this prayer only once and that Matthew recorded more of it than Luke. Others believe that Jesus probably taught the same basic prayer more than once, but not always in the same words. Matthew's version is part of the Sermon on the Mount. In Luke's context of Jesus' final journey to Jerusalem, Jesus visited Martha and Mary's home in Bethany near Jerusalem (10:38-42). Perhaps while He still was in Bethany, a disciple asked Jesus to teach all the disciples how to pray. Jesus responded with a pattern for prayer (11:2-4), a parable that encourages prayer (vv. 5-8), and a promise of answered prayer (vv. 9-13).

Word Study: *Daily*

The Greek word translated **daily** in verse 3, *epiousios,* is one of the few words in the New Testament that does not appear in Greek writings prior to the New Testament. It is found in the New Testament only in the two versions of the Model Prayer (Matt. 6:11; Luke 11:3). After the New Testament, it is not found until a papyrus manuscript of the fifth century A.D. This makes it a challenge to translate. Several possible meanings have been proposed: (1) bread that is essential for existence; (2) bread for tomorrow, that is, bread for the next day; and (3) bread for today. The third meaning is used by most translators.

❖ *Search the Scriptures*

After Jesus finished praying, one of the disciples asked Him to teach them to pray. Jesus taught them *how to pray* with a Model Prayer. He taught them the *need to pray* with the parable of the friend at midnight, and He *encouraged them to pray* by promising that the Father would hear and answer their prayers.

Pray Personally (Luke 11:1-4)

What inspired the disciples to ask Jesus to teach them to pray? Did Jesus intend this to be a prayer to repeat or a pattern for the contents of praying? What are the two main divisions of the prayer? Does verse 2 assume that only God can do these things, or does it assume that we can do them with God's help? Why pray each day for bread? What is the relationship between God's forgiving us and our forgiving others? In what sense does God lead us into temptation?

Verse 1: **And it came to pass, that, as he was praying in a certain place, when he ceased, one of his disciples said unto him, Lord, teach us to pray, as John also taught his disciples.**

The disciples had observed the prayer life of Jesus. It was not unusual for Him to be **praying.** They saw the connection between the life He lived and His prayers to God. Thus **one of his disciples** asked Jesus, **Lord, teach us to pray.** The words **as John also taught his disciples to pray** do not mean to teach them the same prayers or necessarily in the same manner. Rather, the idea of the question was that since John the Baptist taught his disciples to pray, should Jesus not do the same for His disciples?

The request must have thrilled the Lord's heart. The question showed that they were open for Him to teach them a very important lesson. Teachers and parents know that such a question provides a teachable moment for them to impart some important truth to their pupils or children.

Verse 2: **And he said unto them, When ye pray, say, Our Father which art in heaven, Hallowed be thy name. Thy kingdom come. Thy will be done, as in heaven, so in earth.**

One question about this prayer is, Did Jesus intend it to be used word for word as He had given it or was He only giving an example of the elements to be contained in prayer? **When ye pray** implies that He was giving them the elements of prayer. In actual practice, however, both are important. At times reciting the words either alone or together with others is appropriate. This is a good way for a new believer to learn how to pray. The elements of the prayer also provide a model of the kinds of things to include in one's praying.

Usually this is called "the Lord's Prayer," but "the Model Prayer" or "the Disciples' Prayer" are other possible titles. If we call it the Lord's Prayer, we mean the prayer the Lord taught His disciples to pray. Strictly speaking, not every element of this prayer needed to be prayed by Jesus. For example, He never needed to ask for forgiveness of His sins.

Verse 2 focuses on God. It is the **thy** part of the prayer. **Father** is *pater,* a warm family word and a term of respect. The Old Testament seldom refers to God as Father, but Jesus often used this word in reference to His own unique sonship and in referring to the relationship of believers to God. This reminds us that our relationship with God is personal. Only those who come to God through Christ know God as Father. Jesus elaborated on the significance of calling God Father in verses 10-13.

Some people's family experience makes it hard for them to think of God as a loving Father. If their earthly father has been unloving, they cannot appreciate this analogy as much as those whose fathers are loving people who care for their children.

The words **our** and **which art in heaven** are not in the oldest manuscripts of Luke's Gospel and their addition here is clearly an assimilation to the more familiar Matthean form of the prayer found in Matthew 6:9. For this reason neither the *New International Version* nor the *Holman Christian Standard Bible* include the words.

A person's **name** represented the person and his character. God's **name** stands for God and His character. **Hallowed** is *hagiastheto,* which means to "set apart" or "to make holy." Basically this is a petition that God's reputation be such that it matches His actual character—that is, that people and all other beings recognize God for who He is—that "Your name be honored as holy" (HCSB). Believers are expected to speak and to live in ways that God will be recognized as the holy God He is.

Only God can bring in His **kingdom.** We enter His kingdom, bear witness to Him as King, and live in light of the coming kingdom; however, we do not cause His kingdom to **come.** The time and manner of this is in God's hands; we pray for it to happen. God's **kingdom** refers to His reign. In one sense God always has been King; however, the consummation of the kingdom is yet future. Thus we pray for God to bring in His kingdom. Again, the words **Thy will be done, as in heaven, so in earth** are not in the oldest manuscripts of Luke's Gospel and their addition here is clearly an assimilation to the more familiar Matthean form of the prayer found in Matthew 6:10. For this reason neither the *New International Version* nor the *Holman Christian Standard Bible* include the words.

Verse 3: Give us day by day our daily bread.

Verse 3 introduces the **us** part of the Model Prayer. Some people may wonder about moving from the exalted glory and reign of God to the mundane subject of **bread.** But this is basic human need that can only be met by God. **Give us** assumes that our food comes from God; we work for it, but He provides it. Those who live closest to the land know this best. They know that they can plant, cultivate, and harvest; but only God makes the crops grow. Thus this is a prayer of dependence on God and of trust in God.

Although believers do not live by bread alone, but by the Word of God, which feeds our spirits (Deut. 8:3; see Luke 4:4), we also need bread to sustain physical life. Both are gifts from God. The opposite spirit from the spirit of this prayer is exemplified by people who forget God and take credit for whatever they possess (Deut. 8:17; Luke 12:16-21). On the meaning of **daily bread,** see the Word Study at the beginning of this lesson. Saying a blessing before eating is a habit we should continue throughout life.

Verse 4: **And forgive us our sins; for we also forgive everyone that is indebted to us. And lead us not into temptation; but deliver us from evil.**

Forgive us our sins is a prayer that we pray throughout life. This does not mean that believers live a life of sin, but it recognizes that we continue to fall short of the glory of God. John said, "If we say that we have no sin, we deceive ourselves, and the truth is not in us. If we confess our sins, he is faithful and just to forgive us our sins, and to cleanse us from all unrighteousness" (1 John 1:8-9). The paradox is that the closer people are to God, the more aware they are of how far short they fall. At the same time, the further people are from God, the less aware they are of their sins.

Some of God's children fail to confess their sins. Those who live with unconfessed sin cannot know the joy of divine fellowship until they confess and forsake their sins. Thus confession of sins is a prominent and permanent part of Jesus' disciples' prayer lives.

For we also forgive everyone that is indebted to us ties together with the prayer for God to forgive our sins. The relation between God forgiving us and our forgiving others is close. This does not mean that forgiving others makes us worthy for God to forgive us. It means that the spirit that seeks and receives God's forgiveness is the same as the spirit that forgives others. A heart that is open to receive God's forgiveness is open to forgive others. Forgiveness is a two-way street. Jesus' followers receive it, and they give it.

Lead us not into temptation is not easy to explain. James 1:13 makes clear that God is not tempted nor does He tempt others. *Peirasmon* can mean "temptation," "test," or "trial." God sometimes allows us to be tested, but He does not tempt us. This difficult part of the prayer has been translated several ways: "Do not bring us to the time of trial" (NRSV); "Do not put us to the test" (REB); "Keep us from being tempted" (CEV). The idea may be "keep us from yielding to temptation." This would be the opposite of proud people who dare God to put them to the test. Humble people know their weaknesses and ask not to be tested. The words **but deliver us from evil** are not in the oldest manuscripts of Luke's Gospel and their addition here is clearly an assimilation to the more familiar Matthean form of the prayer found in Matthew 6:13. For this reason neither the *New International Version* nor the *Holman Christian Standard Bible* include the words.

One of the mysteries of the Model Prayer is that it does not explicitly include intercessory prayers. Such prayers were practiced by Jesus and taught elsewhere in the New Testament (see Luke 22:32; Acts 12:5; Eph. 6:18-19; Jas. 5:16). Concern for others is implicit in the use of **us** in the Model Prayer.

A pastor said that the most important and the most difficult thing to teach his people was how to pray. Why do you think he felt this way?

Pray Persistently (Luke 11:5-10)

What does the story in verses 5-8 reveal about first-century life? What is the meaning of **importunity?** What are some of the misunderstandings of this parable? Why is true prayer persistent? How did Jesus encourage the disciples to keep on praying? These questions are addressed in comments of verses 5-10.

Verses 5-8: **And he said unto them, Which of you shall have a friend, and shall go unto him at midnight, and say unto him, Friend, lend me three loaves; ⁶for a friend of mine in his journey is come to me, and I have nothing to set before him? ⁷And he from within shall answer and say, Trouble me not: the door is now shut, and my children are with me in bed; I cannot rise and give thee. ⁸I say unto you, Though he will not rise and give him, because he is his friend, yet because of his importunity he will rise and give him as many as he needeth.**

Hospitality was a high priority among first-century Jews. They went out of their way to take care of their guests. Jesus asked the disciples to imagine that they had a good **friend** who arrived as a guest at **midnight** and there was no bread in the house to feed the hungry guest. This would present a dilemma for a Jewish host. He must find bread to feed his friend. He had another **friend** who lived nearby. This neighbor-friend might have bread that he could lend to the frantic host, but the hour was late and the neighbor already was asleep. The host was so desperate that he knocked on his neighbor's door and asked for bread to feed his guest. **Three loaves** were small loaves, but enough for a hungry traveler.

However, the neighbor-friend refused by saying that he and his family were **in bed** and the house was closed up for the night. Many houses in those days were only one room, and sometimes the family slept on one pallet. This may have been the situation here. The neighbor-friend asked his insistent caller not to **trouble** him by asking him to get up and give him the bread he asked for. However, the host kept making the same request until the man got up and loaned him the bread. Jesus said that the man would loan the bread not because the man was **his friend** but **because of his importunity.**

Importunity is *anaideian,* which means "persistence" (NIV, HCSB) or "shamelessness" (NEB). Jesus told a similar parable in 18:1-8. A widow wore down an unjust judge into giving her the justice she sought. What Jesus said of the second parable applied also to the parable of the friend at midnight. "Jesus told his disciples a parable to show them that they should always pray and not give up" (18:1, NIV).

Both of these parables can be easily misunderstood if we assume that the reluctant neighbor or the unjust judge represent God. However, "the point of comparison is not between the neighbor and God but between the petitioner and the disciple. God's response stands in contrast to the neighbor's begrudging help, as 11:9-13 will make clear."[1] Informing or persuading a reluctant god is not the point of these parables.

Why then is prayer to be persistent? (1) When we are concerned deeply about something, we keep praying. For example, if one of your loved ones were desperately ill, no one would have to tell you to keep praying for that person. You would pray repeatedly for the person. We live in a world of needs—our own and others. Concern for needs that only God can meet will result in persistent praying. (2) Because prayer is communion with God. We keep praying not just when we need something but because we daily desire to be with God and to praise and thank Him. (3) Because prayer changes the person who prays regularly. Nothing so transforms a person as spending time each day in prayer. (4) Not only does prayer change the person praying, but God uses our prayers to work out His will in our lives and in the lives of others.

God uses both our service and our prayers. Both are used by God to change us and those for whom we pray. We easily can see the relationship between acts of service and meeting others' needs, but we often fail to see that God uses our prayers to bless and help others.

If your neighbor had some need you could meet, God might lead you to be a good Samaritan and go help the neighbor. But God also wants you to pray for your neighbor. And just as God uses our actions to help others, He also uses our prayers. How prayer works is a mystery. I don't know how God uses our prayers to help someone on the other side of the earth, but I do know that He does. Missionaries testify to it all the time.

Persistent praying does not mean just saying the same words over and over, thinking that will influence God. Jesus said that such mindless repetition is used by pagans, not believers. Jesus spoke of the importance of a place where we can pray our personal prayers (Matt. 6:6). The Bible encourages the kind of daily prayers that were practiced by Daniel (Dan. 6:10).

Verses 9-10: **And I say unto you, Ask, and it shall be given you; seek, and ye shall find; knock, and it shall be opened unto you. [10]For everyone that asketh receiveth; and he that seeketh findeth; and to him that knocketh it shall be opened.**

Verse 9 is a call to prayer based on the parable in verses 5-8. Verse 10 is a promise that God will answer prayer. Jesus used three words to describe praying: **ask ... seek ... knock.** The present tense of these three imperatives indicates continuous action: "keep on asking," "keep on seeking," "keep on knocking." In a sense, Jesus used different words to describe the same reality. His point was to keep praying and God will hear your prayers.

Ask (*aiteite*) often is used of asking in prayer: "Ye have not, because ye ask not. Ye ask, and receive not, because ye ask amiss, that ye may consume it upon your lusts" (Jas. 4:2-3). Someone has used this analogy to show how these three words are illustrated in a child's request of his mother or father. If a child is with his mother, he asks. If he does not know where she is, he seeks her. If he hears her in a room with a closed door, he knocks.

Verse 9 is the challenge to pray persistently; verse 10 is the promise that God will hear our prayers. Jesus promised, "For everyone who asks receives; and he who seeks finds; and to him who knocks, the door will be opened" (NIV). Jesus' promise is not a blank check, however. "Jesus assumed that such prayer would be in accordance with God's will and would include an implied 'yet not my will, but yours be done' (Luke 22:42)."[2] Verse 13 further clarifies that the all-wise and all-loving God, our Heavenly Father, knows what we really need when we pray.

Pray Confidently (Luke 11:11-13)

Why do so many people doubt that God answers prayer? Why do we believe that God does answer prayer? In what ways are earthly fathers like the Heavenly Father? These questions are addressed in comments on verses 11-13.

Verses 11-13: **If a son shall ask bread of any of you that is a father, will he give him a stone? or if he ask a fish, will he for a fish give him a serpent? [12]Or if he shall ask an egg, will he offer him a scorpion? [13]If ye then, being evil, know how to give good gifts unto your children: how much more shall your heavenly Father give the Holy Spirit to them that ask him?**

Jesus compared the Heavenly Father to earthly fathers. Jesus asked what a **father** would do if his **son** asked for **bread.** No decent father would **give him**

a stone. If his **son** asked for **a fish,** no decent father would substitute **a serpent.** Or if the son asked for **an egg,** no decent father would give him **a scorpion.** When a **scorpion** is curled up, his shape is like that of **an egg.** No loving parents would give their children what would harm them. Instead, they give their children what will help them.

Compared to the **heavenly Father,** earthly fathers are **evil.** If imperfect parents seek **to give good gifts unto** their **children,** Jesus asked, **how much more shall your heavenly Father give the Holy Spirit to them that ask him?** Notice the words **how much more.** The parable in verses 5-8 is a "how much more" parable. So is the parable of the unjust judge in 18:1-8. If a sleeping man will give his persistent neighbor bread at midnight, how much more will the loving Father give His children what they ask? If an unjust judge will hear the requests of a persistent widow, how much more will the loving Father hear our prayers?

The best of all the **good gifts** that the **heavenly Father** gives is the **Holy Spirit,** the gift of His abiding presence with the one who prays. Parents want to be there for their children. However, we discover that we cannot always be there for them. But we can entrust them to the care and presence of the Heavenly Father, who is always there for all His children.

These verses encourage us to pray with the assurance that God will answer our prayers. Why do so many people complain that when they prayed God did not answer their prayers? Some people have a limited definition of prayer and of answers to their prayers. They think of praying solely as asking God for something, and they think of answers to prayer as God giving them exactly what they want when they want it. Prayer is much more than petition. Jesus was not promising that God would give anyone who asks whatever the person asks for and give it in the way the person expects. He promised that God is a loving, wise Father who gives His children what they need.

The prayers of some people are not answered because those praying are not in a right relation with the Father. Those who cherish sin in their hearts will not be heard by God (Ps. 66:18). God does not answer the prayers of people who mistreat others (Isa. 1:15). He does not hear proud prayers (Luke 18:9-14).

The Bible contains many examples of people whose prayers seemed at first not to be answered but actually were answered in God's way and on His schedule. To some requests, the Father says, "No." To some, He says, "Later." Paul prayed for God to remove the thorn in the flesh. God did not remove it, but Paul felt that God had answered him (2 Cor. 12:7-10). God often answers our prayers in unexpected ways. Paul wanted to preach in Rome. He asked the Roman believers to pray that he could do that. Paul did get to Rome, but he arrived as a prisoner (Acts 28; Rom. 15:19-24).

Sometimes even people of faith ask for something that God knows will harm them. Elijah was a mighty man of prayer, but when he was under the juniper tree, he asked God to take his life (1 Kings 19:4). God did not honor this foolish request, but He answered the prayer. He sent an angel to feed Elijah and led him to be renewed.

Praying must be done in faith, which not only believes that God is able to answer our prayers but also trusts Him to answer as a loving Father who has our best interests at heart. Just as a wise and loving father does not give his child something that will hurt the child or that the child does not need, so does our Heavenly Father give us good things that we need.

> Have faith in God when your pray'rs are unanswered,
> Your earnest plea He will never forget;
> Wait on the Lord, trust His Word and be patient,
> Have faith in God, He'll answer yet.[3]

❖ Spiritual Transformations

One of the disciples asked Jesus to teach them to pray. Jesus answered in three ways. First, He gave the Model Prayer to teach them how to pray. Second, He told the parable of the friend at midnight to teach them to be persistent in their praying. Third, Jesus encouraged them to pray by promising that the Father would hear and answer their prayers.

How did you learn to pray? _____

When you pray, how many of the following elements do you include in your praying? Praise __ Thanks __ Confession __ Petition __ Intercession __

What have you found is the best time and place for you to have your personal prayers? _____

Prayer of Commitment: "Father, Your name be honored as holy.
> Your kingdom come.
> Give us each day our daily bread.
> And forgive us our sins,
>> for we ourselves also forgive everyone in debt to us.
> And do not bring us into temptation" (Luke 11:2-4; HCSB).

[1]Bock, *Luke 9:51- 24:53*, 1060.
[2]Stein, "Luke," NAC, 328.
[3]B. B. McKinney, "Have Faith in God," No. 405, *The Baptist Hymnal*, 1991.

FINDING FORGIVENESS

Background Passage: Luke 15:1-32
Focal Passage: Luke 15:11-24
Key Verse: Luke 15:20b

❖ *Significance of the Lesson*

• The *Theme* of this lesson is God rejoices in the return of the penitent.
• The *Life Question* this lesson seeks to address is If I repent, will God forgive me—even if I have sinned greatly?
• The *Biblical Truth* is that God will forgive repentant people.
• The *Life Impact* is to help you repent and seek God's forgiveness when you sin.

Sin, Repentance, and Forgiveness

In the secular worldview, people have little concept of sin and repentance. Anything goes, and whatever gratifies self is not only permissible but is also to be pursued by any means. When confronted with the gospel, some of these people will be convicted of their sin; but many of them will fail to repent. Sometimes they are unwilling to turn from their sins. At other times, they doubt that God will forgive their sins.

The biblical worldview holds that God is loving and gracious. When unbelievers repent of their sins, God forgives their sins and accepts them as His children. He deeply wants people to seek and accept His forgiveness.

The Three Parables of Luke 15:1-32

Luke 15 will be in any list of favorite chapters of the Bible. It contains three of Jesus' most familiar parables: the lost coin, the lost sheep, and the prodigal son. The latter is the most famous of these parables. Although it is generally called the parable of the prodigal son, a more inclusive name would be the parable of the loving father. Two background facts help in studying Luke 15:11-24: (1) The key to all three parables is the setting in verses 1-2. The scribes and Pharisees were criticizing Jesus for eating with tax collectors and sinners. Jesus told three stories to support His attitude toward sinners.

All three illustrate God's joy in receiving repentant sinners. (2) Luke 15:11-24 is only half of the third parable. The parable focuses on the loving father, and he had two lost sons. The younger son represents sinners who repent. The father represents God who receives repentant sinners. The elder brother represents the Pharisees who were critical of God's mercy for sinners.

Word Study: *Riotous*

The word translated **riotous** in verse 13 is *asotos*. It comes from the word for "save" (*sozo*) preceded by the negative *a*. It means something or someone who "is not saved." The only use of this adverb in the New Testament is in Luke 15:13, where it is used with the word *zao* ("live," "living"). Here it refers to the kind of dissolute living practiced by the younger son, who went to the limit of sinful excesses. The related noun *asotia* means "debauchery," "dissipation," "profligacy," or "reckless living" (see Eph. 5:18).

❖ *Search the Scriptures*

Jesus probably had withdrawn from Judea and had moved into Perea. In the course of His ministry in Perea, the Pharisees and the teachers of the Law complained because He welcomed sinners and ate with them (Luke 15:1). In His defense, Jesus told three parables about celebrating the recovery of what had been lost. The short story in Luke 15:11-32 is the clincher in His defense of His accepting all people.

Jesus told a parable of a loving father who desperately wanted to reclaim two lost sons. The younger son wanted his father to give him his portion of his inheritance. When the father did this, the son left home and lived a sinful life in a distant land. When his money ran out and a famine came, he ended up feeding pigs. The son came to his senses and realized that he would be better off as a hired servant in his father's house. Therefore, he decided to return home, confess his sins, and ask no more than to be treated as a hired servant. The father ran to greet him and called for a welcome home feast, declaring that his lost son had been found and his dead son was alive again.

Rebellion (Luke 15:11-13)

Why did the son ask for his inheritance while his father was still living? Why did the father give it to him? What does this reveal about human freedom of choice? What does it teach about sin?

Verses 11-12: **And he said, A certain man had two sons:** [12]**And the younger of them said to his father, Father, give me the portion of goods that falleth to me. And he divided unto them his living.**

The **certain man** in this parable was a father who had **two sons.** The father is the key person in the parable. The father's relationship with his **younger** son is featured in verses 11-24; the older son is featured in verses 25-32. As already noted, each son was lost—one in the far country and the other at home. As Leslie D. Weatherhead said, "The story, then, is the story of a loving father who had two boys, one of whom walled himself off from his father's love by doing evil; while the other walled himself off from that same love by doing good."[1]

The story begins with the request of the younger son to his father, **Give me the portion of goods that falleth to me** ("my share of the estate," NIV). The father **divided unto them his living** ("divided his property between them," NIV). What portion did each son receive? The Old Testament Law said that a father of two sons should give his older son twice as much of his inheritance (Deut. 21:17). Was this a normal way for fathers to pass along their inheritance to their sons? Later Jewish sources give more detailed instructions about inheritances, and from these we learn that "if a man decided to make gifts, he normally gave the capital but retained the income. He could then no longer dispose of the capital, only of his interest in the income. But the recipient could get nothing until the death of the giver. . . . We see this in the elder brother. The father clearly retained the management of the property and the use of the proceeds. But he can say, 'all that is mine is yours' (v. 31). The son of Sirach thought it unwise to give property away too early and he warns against it (Ecclus. 33:19-21). But his warning shows that the practice existed. What is unusual about the son's request is that he sought the use of the capital immediately."[2]

Keep in mind that Jesus' parables were realistic in setting but often contained surprises. Two surprises in verse 12 are the son's request to receive his inheritance while his father was alive and the father's decision to give it to him.

The parable is not about how sons and fathers ought to act. Jesus obviously intended the father to represent the actions of God the Father and the son to represent sinners. What does this reveal about God? It shows that God has given human beings the wonderful and terrible gift of freedom. He made us free to choose to go to the far country. God knew that this gift of freedom was fraught with peril, but He also knew that only as people are free can they choose to love Him. If we are free to love Him, we also are free not to love Him.

What does this reveal about sin? The son's actions are not so hard to understand. As children mature, it is normal for them to move from dependence on their parents to independence. This is normal and healthy for human beings. Many youth yearn for that time to come, and many seek freedom before they are mature enough to make wise decisions. At the same time, we can understand how the immature insistence of the younger son represents the basic sin of turning from God to go our own way. That in fact is the basic sin—turning from God to seek our own way.

The Bible teaches that all have sinned: "All we like sheep have gone astray; we have turned every one to his own way" (Isa. 53:6). This basic sin is manifest in a variety of ways. Some commit the kind of sins of which the younger son was guilty. Others commit the kind of sins of which the elder brother was guilty (self-righteousness, lovelessness).

Verse 13: And not many days after the younger son gathered all together, and took his journey into a far country, and there wasted his substance with riotous living.

Not many days after means "soon." In technical jargon, Luke used a recognized figure of speech in which the negation (**not**) of the opposite (**many days**) expresses what is meant—"a few days after." Probably the only thing that delayed him was the need to turn all his inheritance into cash. *Synagagon panta* (**gathered all together**) means either that he "turned the whole of his share into cash" (REB) or "packed up everything he owned" (CEV). **Took his journey into a far country** ("set off for a distant country," NIV) shows that he was lured by the anticipated pleasures of the **far country**. His way of life in the far country is summed up in two actions: he **wasted his substance** ("squandered his wealth," NIV) and he did this in **riotous living** ("wild living," NIV). Sin does offer a kind of pleasure, but it is superficial and short-lived.

Like many people today, he assumed that money can buy happiness. Most people know the old saying that money won't buy happiness, but most people don't really believe it. They assume that if they had enough money, they would be able to afford the good life. We are not told the specific ways the younger son spent his money. His older brother accused him of "living with harlots" (v. 30). We cannot tell whether that was true or whether it is what the older son would have done if he had been in the far country.

The fact that the younger son was in **a far country** made it easier to do as he pleased. Likely he was in a Gentile country, since verses 15-16 show that pigs were raised there. He was away from home and in a place where no one knew him. Thus he felt that he could live as he chose. When people travel to distant places where they are not known, some people do things that they would not do in their own communities.

Suppose for a moment that you had met the younger son at the front gate as he was about to leave home for the far country. Could you have talked him out of going? I doubt if anyone could. When people have the gleam of the far country in their eyes, warnings usually are ignored.

Ruin (Luke 15:14-16)

What did the younger son expect to find in the far country? To what degree did he find it? What surprises did he experience? In what way does his experience teach us about the consequences of turning from our Heavenly Father?

Verses 14-16: And when he had spent all, there arose a mighty famine in that land; and he began to be in want. ¹⁵And he went and joined himself to a citizen of that country; and he sent him into his fields to feed swine. ¹⁶And he would fain have filled his belly with the husks that the swine did eat: and no man gave unto him.

The fact that he so quickly **had spent all** was probably a surprise to the younger son. One mark of his immaturity was his assumption that he had enough money to live any way he chose and to do it indefinitely. However, his money was soon gone because he squandered it. At the same time that his money ran out, **there arose a mighty famine in that land.** His personal financial crisis was made worse by the famine that came. This probably was also a surprise to him. He was not ready to face either crisis.

As a result of his wasteful spending and the famine, **he began to be in want** ("in need," NIV). **Want** is *hustereisthai*, which means "to go without." He was in desperate need—as verses 15-16 show. In our use of the words, *wants* are things we would like to have, and *needs* are things which we must have to survive. One of the sins of modern American society is that we are constantly moving things from the "want" list to the "need" list.

The younger son was in need of the basics to sustain life. He was gradually starving to death. Two things show his desperate plight. For one thing, the only job he could find was feeding **swine** ("pigs," NIV). This was an abomination to Jews. Those who first heard Jesus tell this story would have felt feeding pigs was the worst thing he could have done. Second, his plight was so serious that **he would fain have filled his belly with the husks** ("pods," NIV) **that the swine did eat.** The pigs' diet was "carob pods" (HCSB), which only pigs and the poorest people ate. But the younger son was denied even these things—**no man gave unto him.** This may mean that the owner of the pigs would not allow him to eat any of the food for the pigs. It also is a sad reminder that his former "friends" ignored his plight.

Thus the young man's dreams of pleasure and fulfillment in the far country turned into a nightmare. Marvin R. Vincent described three famous paintings of the prodigal son in the far country. Each portrays the inherent dangers of his pleasures and the certain ruin toward which he was headed. A painting by the young Teniers in the Louvre shows the young man at a tavern with two prostitutes. In the background is a poor old beggar woman pleading for alms and a pigsty where a stable-boy is feeding swine. Holbein pictures the prodigal feasting with his mistress and gambling with someone sharper than he, who is sweeping money off the table. Jan Steen pictures him in a garden before an inn. Two children are blowing bubbles, symbolizing transient pleasures and that the bubble of his life was about to burst.[3]

The Bible teaches that we reap whatever we sow (Gal. 6:7). Some might defend the younger son's time in the far country by saying, "A young man has to sow his wild oats." They overlook that if he sows wild oats, he will reap the fruit of the wild oats.

Repentance (Luke 15:17-20a)

What caused the younger son to decide to go home? How does his experience illustrate repentance?

Verses 17-20a: **And when he came to himself, he said, How many hired servants of my father's have bread enough and to spare, and I perish with hunger!** [18]**I will arise and go to my father, and will say unto him, Father, I have sinned against heaven, and before thee.** [19]**And am no more worthy to be called thy son: make me as one of thy hired servants.** [20a]**And he arose, and came to his father.**

The son's condition in the pigpen shows that he had reached bottom. Some people have to hit bottom before they recognize their need to change. Jesus said, **he came to himself** ("came to his senses," NIV, HCSB). "This refers not only to a mental process that causes him to think more clearly about his situation but also to a moral renewal involving repentance."[4] He was like a person who had lost his mind and had now regained it. For the first time he saw himself as he really was. In other words, he was convicted of his sins and he saw his desperate plight.

He was not only repelled by his sorry state, but he was attracted by his memories of living in his **father's** house. His father was kind and generous not only to his sons but also to his servants. **Hired servants** were the lowest rank of those who served the father. They were hired by the day, thus they lacked the security of those employed full time. The son realized that he would be much better off as a day-servant than he was now. They had **bread enough and to spare.** Yet he reflected, **I perish with hunger! Perish** is *apollumai,* which often is used to describe the spiritual death of sinners (John 3:16; 2 Pet. 3:9). This word was used in Luke 15 of the lostness of the sheep, the coin, and the younger son (vv. 4,6,24). He was not only dying physically, but he was dying in every other way also. Those who stay in the far country are lost and dying morally and spiritually. Recognizing that fact can be the first step toward their repentance and redemption.

Repentance begins with recognizing one's sins and remembering the Father's love, but it must include a decision to act. The younger son made a decision: **I will arise and go to my father.** Repentance and faith involve an act of will, not just feelings of remorse and conviction. He decided to go home. He also planned what he could say when he arrived home. This constitutes the confession that accompanies true repentance—**I have sinned against heaven, and before thee.** He realized that he had acted selfishly and indifferently toward his father who loved him, but he knew that all sin is ultimately against God (**against heaven).** That is what makes it sin.

We speak of an age of accountability when people become accountable to God for their wrong actions and attitudes. A young child usually learns the difference between good behavior and bad behavior. At some point, a child realizes that disobeying parents is wrong. This stops short of accountability to God, which comes when the child or youth realizes that disobedience to parents and other bad things are sins—that is, they are wrong not only because they hurt others but also because they hurt God and break His commandments.

Another aspect of repentance is awareness that we are **no more worthy** of God's love. We cannot come to God claiming that He must accept us because of our goodness and merit. The younger son knew that he could not ask his father to receive him based on the good he had done. The elder brother tried to base his acceptance on that basis (v. 29), but he was not worthy because of his lack of fellowship with his father and his refusal of his brother. Those who expect God to accept and reward them for their good works need to take a closer look at themselves and their relationships to God and to others.

The son acted on the basis of his inner decision—**and he arose, and came to his father.** Good intentions do not save people from their sins. Repentance is conviction, contrition, and decision within; but if these are real, they will involve turning from sin and turning to God. Visualize the younger son as he left the far country. He looks wasted and haggard of body, but there is a look of determination and even hope in his eyes. He has been far from home, but now he is on his way home.

I've wandered far away from God, Now I'm coming home;
The paths of sin too long I've trod, Lord, I'm coming home.
Coming home, coming home, Never more to roam,
Open wide Thine arms of love, Lord, I'm coming home.[5]

Reception (Luke 15:20b-24)

What does this parable reveal about God's attitude toward lost sinners? What does it reveal about God's response to repentant sinners? If the father loved his son, why did he not go to the far country and bring his son home? What do these verses reveal about forgiveness?

Verse 20b: **But when he was yet a great way off, his father saw him, and had compassion, and ran, and fell on his neck, and kissed him.**

This one line reveals much about the father in the parable and therefore much about our Heavenly Father. The father **saw** his son **when he was yet a great** ("long," NIV, HCSB) **way off.** This shows two things about the father, in addition to his long-range vision. It shows that he must have spent much time looking down the road and hoping to see his son. This, I believe, was evidence of his love and prayers that his son would come home. He had been grieved by the son's leaving home. He prayed and yearned for him to come home.

The first two parables in this chapter describe seeking the lost sheep and the lost coin. In both of those parables, the lost was sought until found. In this parable, why did the concerned father not go to the far country and bring his son home? There is no question that God seeks sinners. He sought Adam and Eve after their sin in the garden of Eden (Gen. 3:9). He sent His Son to seek and to save the lost (Luke 19:10). The Bible is the story of a loving God seeking sinners. Why then did this father, who represents God in the parable, not seek his lost son?

No parable can reveal every truth. The father did not go and bring his son home because he knew that his son was a person, not a sheep or a lost coin. All the shepherd had to do was to find the lost sheep, pick it up, and carry it home. But lost people are not animals that God can pick up and carry into His arms of love. For people to come home, they must decide to come home. Verse 20, however, shows us that the father had been waiting and longing for his erring son to come home. Stanley Jones told of a mother who went to the "far country" to seek her wayward daughter: She took some photographs of herself and wrote on the back of each one, "Come home," and signed each one "Mother." She placed these photographs in the kinds of places where her daughter might be. The girl saw one of them, read the short note, and went home.[6]

Finally the father's prayers were answered. As he looked down the road, he recognized a familiar figure while he was still a long way from the front gate. Then the father **ran** to where the boy was. This was something that older men did not do in that day. But this father could not wait for his son to reach him; he ran to greet him. When the father reached the son, he **fell on his neck, and kissed him.** These were signs of deep emotion and loving acceptance. The father acted out of **compassion.** This is the same word for compassion (*esplanchnisthe*) that described Jesus in Matthew 9:36 and the good Samaritan in Luke 10:33. It is the word expressing deep emotion and commitment to help the one in need.

Verses 21-24: **And the son said unto him, Father, I have sinned against heaven, and in thy sight, and am no more worthy to be called thy son. [22]But the father said to his servants, Bring forth the best robe, and put it on him; and put a ring on his hand, and shoes on his feet: [23]and bring hither the fatted calf, and kill it; and let us eat, and be merry: [24]for this my son was dead, and is alive again; he was lost, and is found. And they began to be merry.**

Verse 21 is the son's confession. He began to say the words that he had planned to say (vv. 18-19). He confessed his sin against his father and against God. He stated that he was **no more** ("no longer," NIV, HCSB) **worthy to be called thy son.** But that was as far as he got in his plea. He was not able to finish his confession as he had planned it. Apparently this was because the father interrupted the son's confession with his own words of welcome. We are not told what **the father** said to his returned son. Instead, we hear what he **said to his servants** in the hearing of his son. He told them to do four things: (1) **Bring forth the best robe, and put it on him.** (2) **Put a ring on his hand.** (3) Put **shoes on his feet.** (4) **Bring hither the fatted calf, and kill it; and let us eat, and be merry.**

All of these things were signs of honoring and welcoming the son. The father's actions revealed several things: (1) his acceptance of his repentant son as a son, not as a servant; (2) his joy over his son's return; and (3) his forgiveness of the hurt inflicted on him by his son.

Seldom did most people eat a **fatted calf.** But the joyful father did all he could to show all that he was overjoyed with the return of his son. His joy was like the joy in heaven symbolized by finding the lost sheep (v. 7) and the lost coin (v. 10). This joy of God over the repentance of one sinner is the explicit theme of all three parables in Luke 15. His joy stands in marked contrast to the attitude of the elder brother in verses 25-32.

The father's reason for greeting the returned son with such joy is stated in verse 24, and substantially repeated in verse 32—**my son was dead, and is alive again; he was lost, and is found.** Sinners are **lost** because they are away from God. Most lost people would object to being called *lost.* They believe they know where they are, but the fact is that they are lost from the love and care of God. Jesus used the word **lost** to describe the sheep (v. 4) and the coin (v. 9) as well as the returned son. Jesus came to seek and to save the lost (19:10). This search led Him to Calvary on our behalf. Jesus also had the father refer to his returned son as one who **was dead, and is alive again.** Lost people surely would object to being called **dead.** Elsewhere Jesus referred to passing from death unto life in a spiritual sense (John 5:24). And Paul described sinners as spiritually dead and made alive in Christ (Eph. 2:1-5).

> Ring the bells of heaven! There is joy today,
> For a soul, returning from the wild!
> See, the Father meets him out upon the way,
> Welcoming His weary, wand'ring child.[7]

❖ *Spiritual Transformations*

The younger son's request for his inheritance typifies the basic human sin of misusing the God-given gift of freedom to turn from God into our own ways. The actions of the son in the far country and their results show the consequences of rebelling against God. The son's decision and action in returning home show what repentance is. The father's welcome shows God's joy in welcoming and forgiving sinners.

With what part of the parable can you personally identify? _____

The truths of this parable apply to the lost who have never sought the Lord and to believers who have gone astray and who need to return to the Father. If you are in either of these situations, *will you confess your sins to God and accept His forgiveness?* _____

Prayer of Commitment: God, I thank You for loving me and for forgiving me when I repent of my sins.

[1]Leslie D. Weatherhead, *In Quest of a Kingdom,* 87.

[2]Leon Morris, *The Gospel According to St. Luke,* in The Tyndale New Testament Commentaries [Grand Rapids: William B. Eerdmans Publishing Company, 1974], 240. Note: The abbreviation "Ecclus." is not a reference to the biblical book Ecclesiastes but to the intertestamental book Ecclesiasticus or The Wisdom of Jesus Son of Sirach (Ben Sira).

[3]Marvin R. Vincent, *Word Studies in the New Testament,* vol. 1 [Grand Rapids: William B. Eerdmans Publishing Company, 1946], 389.

[4]Stein, "Luke," NAC, 406.

[5]William J. Kirkpatrick, "Lord, I'm Coming Home," No. 309, *The Baptist Hymnal,* 1991.

[6]Cited by John A. Redhead, *Getting to Know God* [Nashville: Abingdon Press, 1954], 59.

[7]William O. Cushing, "Ring the Bells of Heaven," No. 428, *The Baptist Hymnal,* 1991.

EXPERIENCING ETERNAL LIFE

Background Passage: John 11:1-54
Focal Passage: John 11:20-27,38-45
Key Verses: John 11:25-26

❖ *Significance of the Lesson*

• The *Theme* of this week's lesson is that life and resurrection are in Jesus.

• The *Life Question* this lesson seeks to address is How can I experience true life both here and hereafter?

• The *Biblical Truth* is that only Jesus, who is the resurrection and the life, can give people true life through a relationship with Him and can effect their resurrection to eternal life for the hereafter.

• The *Life Impact* is to help you live your life based on and consistent with the eternal life you have received from the One who is the resurrection and the life.

Different Definitions of Life

In materialistic worldviews, this present life is all people have; nothing lies beyond the span of physical existence. Thus people's lives often revolve around getting as much as they can while they can of money, pleasure, power—whatever secures even momentary happiness. Always in the background—feared, denied, covered up—death lurks. Pessimism, fatalism, and hopelessness characterize many people's lives—and they have no hope beyond the grave.

The biblical worldview declares that Jesus is the resurrection and the life. He raises to new life people who repent of their sins and place their faith in Him. He offers them true life now and never-ending life with Him beyond physical death. Eternal life that is qualitative and quantitative is found only in Jesus. Because of His life-giving power, people who enter a relationship with Him have hope and life in the present and will experience resurrection to eternal life in the future.

Word Study: *The Resurrection, and the Life*

According to John 11:25, Jesus said that He is **the resurrection, and the life. Resurrection** is *anastasis,* which means "to rise" from the dead. **Life** is *zoe.* This key word is found 36 times in the Gospel of John, more than in any other book of the New Testament. *Zoe* is more than mere biological life. It is true life, spiritual life. In John's Gospel it often is preceded by the word "eternal" (*aionion*). The linking of **resurrection** and **life** points to the fact that the life Jesus brings is the life of the age to come. But Jesus does more than *bring* resurrection and life, He *is* **the resurrection, and the life.** Before calling Himself **the life,** Jesus first called Himself **the resurrection.** This reminds us that the whole human race is dead in trespasses and sins. It reminds us that no one will possess life unless he or she is first raised from the dead. It reminds us that Christ is the beginning of life. And thus it reminds us that restoration from death must precede the state of life.

❖ *Search the Scriptures*

Although Martha regretted that Jesus had not come in time to heal her brother Lazarus, she had faith in Jesus and hope of a future resurrection. Jesus told her that He is the resurrection and the life, who gives eternal life to believers. Martha confessed faith in Jesus as the Messiah and Son of God. Although Lazarus had been dead for four days, Jesus called him back from death to life.

Affirmation of Confidence (John 11:20-24)

What do we know about Martha and Mary? What had happened in verses 1-19? Was Martha's greeting to Jesus in verse 21 a rebuke or a regret? What view of the resurrection did Martha have? These questions will be answered with a review of the background in verses 1-19 and in an examination of verses 20-24.

Verse 20: Then Martha, as soon as she heard that Jesus was coming, went and met him: but Mary sat still in the house.

Martha and **Mary** are mentioned in verse 20. What do we know about these two women from other passages? They were sisters in whose home Jesus visited in Luke 10:38-42. In John 11:1-2 we learn that the sisters had a brother Lazarus. The three are mentioned again in John 12:1-9, where Martha was serving a meal and Mary anointed Jesus with an expensive ointment, for which she was commended by Jesus.

John 11:1-3 shows that the sisters sent word for Jesus to come because Lazarus was sick. Jesus was in Perea when He received the message (10:40-42). He remained there for two more days before He told His disciples that the sickness of Lazarus, whom He loved, would be for the glory of God (11:4-6). After two days Jesus said that they were returning to Judea (v. 7). The disciples reminded Him of the danger of going where His enemies planned to kill Him (v. 8). Jesus replied that He was walking in the light (vv. 9-10). Then He told them that Lazarus was dead (vv. 11-15). Thomas said that they would go with Jesus even though this might result in their deaths (vv. 16-17). Because Bethany was less than two miles from Jerusalem, many of the Jews had come to mourn with the two sisters (vv. 18-19).

Martha was the first to go out to meet Jesus when she heard He was near. **Mary** stayed **in the house** with the mourners.

Verses 21-22: **Then said Martha unto Jesus, Lord, if thou hadst been here, my brother had not died. [22]But I know, that even now, whatsoever thou wilt ask of God, God will give it thee.**

Martha's first words to Jesus were, **Lord, if thou hadst been here, my brother had not died** ("would not have died," NIV). Was this a rebuke to Jesus for not coming in time to heal Lazarus or a statement of regret without any blame placed on Jesus? Since Lazarus had been dead for four days when Jesus arrived in Bethany, Jesus probably could not have gotten there in time even if He had left when He first received the message to come help. The distance from Perea to Bethany was a two-day journey. Thus the message would have taken two days to reach Jesus and Jesus would have been on the road for the next two days (four days in all).

Whether or not Martha expressed frustration tinged with blame, other people in similar circumstances do complain to God that He did not respond to their prayers when they most needed help. God does not operate on our time schedule; He acts in His own time and way. If we give Martha the benefit of the doubt, she was only expressing a regret, not a rebuke to Jesus. Even if it was a rebuke, Jesus did not rebuke her in turn for it. He knew that it was the natural way for a sister to feel.

One reason for believing her words in verse 21 were only an expression of regret is what she said in verse 22. She said she believed that **whatsoever** Jesus asked **of God** would be given to Him. Did she expect Jesus to raise Lazarus from the dead? Her later words and actions do not support this interpretation. Her words "must not be read as her belief that Jesus could reverse the reality of death (cf. 11:39). Instead, her statement should be understood as indicating a strong confidence in Jesus' relationship with the

Father and that in spite of her resignation to Lazarus's death, somehow Jesus would understand the plight of the mourning sisters as well as the general nature of Lazarus's future hope."[1]

Verses 23-24: **Jesus saith unto her, Thy brother shall rise again. [24]Martha saith unto him, I know that he shall rise again in the resurrection at the last day.**

Jesus assured Martha that her **brother shall rise again.** His words in verses 25-26 and His actions in verses 43-44 show that Jesus meant more than Martha realized at the time. She assumed that Jesus was speaking of the future resurrection of the righteous dead **at the last day.** This resurrection hope was fairly common among the rank-and-file people. Her belief offered her some comfort in her present sorrow. But she thought of the resurrection as a future event, not as a person to whom she was speaking. She may or may not have heard of others whom Jesus had raised from the dead. He had restored life to the daughter of Jairus (Matt. 9:18-19,23-26; Mark 5:21-24, 35-43; Luke 8:40-42,49-56) and to the son of the widow of Nain (Luke 7: 11-17). However, even if she knew of these, she probably saw Lazarus as more hopeless because he had been dead four days, whereas the other two had been dead only a short time. Some sources indicate that the Jews believed that a dead person's spirit might return to the body during the first three days, but they considered a person hopelessly dead by the fourth day.

The sisters' grief is a grief shared by all of humanity. At some point in life each of us feels the deep sense of loss from the death of someone we love. Only faith gives adequate support for the grieving, and Christian hope is the only true basis for confidence of the continuing life of the dead in Christ and offers the only true comfort for the bereaved. Paul wrote to the Thessalonians and stated that they do not "grieve like the rest of men, who have no hope" (1 Thess. 4:13, NIV). Christians are human and grieve, but their grief is eased by their hope.

Herschel H. Hobbs, the founding author of this quarterly commentary and the one in whose honor it is now named, wrote about his experience with his wife's death: "When my wife and I had been married fifty-seven and one-half years she learned she was terminally ill. At that time she asked me the most difficult question I have ever tried to answer. She asked, 'Am I dying?' I said, 'Yes, darling.' 'Why?' she asked. I told her I did not know. Then I said, 'All I can tell you is that I will hold your hand as long as I can, and when I can go no farther, Jesus' hand will take hold and lead you through.' She never asked again. She never complained. Her only concern was for those left behind."[2]

Pronouncement of Life (John 11:25-26)

What new revelation did these verses make? In what sense is Jesus **the resurrection, and the life**? What is the relationship between this claim and the resurrection of Jesus? To what groups do His promises apply? These questions are addressed in comments on verses 25-26.

Verses 25-26: Jesus said unto her, I am the resurrection, and the life: he that believeth in me, though he were dead, yet shall he live: [26]**and whosoever liveth and believeth in me shall never die. Believest thou this?**

This is one of the high points of divine revelation. No one else but Jesus could make such a claim. Jesus corrected Martha's belief in several ways. For one thing, she saw resurrection as only *future,* but Jesus spoke of it as *present.* She thought of it as *an event,* but He spoke of it as *a person.*

Jesus is the One who gives life—real, abundant, and eternal. The word for **life** (*zoe*) is found 36 times in John's Gospel, and most of them cluster around something Jesus said or did. Our life is in Him. The important thing about this **life** is that it is life, not merely existence. Eternal life is everlasting, but everlasting existence without God would be a description of hell, not of heaven. **Life** in Christ is a personal relationship with the living God (17:3).

The words **he that believeth in me, though he were dead, yet shall he live** are Jesus' promise that the dead in Christ are alive, not dead or unconscious. At times, Jesus used the word *sleep* to describe death (see 11:11). However, He did not mean that the spirit was not alive. To put it more clearly: "he who believes in me will live, even though he dies" (NIV). This promise applied to Lazarus as one who had died in faith. Lazarus was dead, but Jesus said that Lazarus was still living. Although Lazarus was physically dead and not with the sisters on earth, he was alive!

Further, this life begins when one comes to know Jesus Christ, not after a person dies. This is the emphasis of verse 26: **Whosoever liveth and believeth in me shall never die.** Jesus did not deny that each believer will experience physical death, but He emphasized that eternal life begins with faith and that death only opens a new dimension of that life.

This great promise pointed forward to Jesus' own victory over death when He was raised from the dead. Jesus and His resurrection are the basis for Christian hope in the face of death. Because of His victory over death, we, with the apostle Paul, can say, "O death, where is thy sting? O grave, where is thy victory? The sting of death is sin; and the strength of sin is the law. But thanks be to God, which giveth us the victory through our Lord Jesus Christ" (1 Cor. 15:55-57).

Jesus' miracles of restoring dead people to life during His ministry pointed ahead to His unique victory. Each of the people He restored from death to life later died. But Jesus was raised from the dead as the victor over death. He never will die. He has the keys of death and the grave. Death has no more dominion over Him.

Believest thou this? or "Do you believe this?" (NIV, HCSB). Jesus asked Martha this key question because faith is necessary to know the life that Jesus is and that He came to bring.

Confession of Faith (John 11:27)

What are the arguments of those who believe that Martha's response to Jesus was an inadequate confession of faith? What are the arguments of those who believe Martha's response to Jesus was a strong confession of faith? These questions are addressed in comments on verse 27.

Verse 27: **She saith unto him, Yea, Lord: I believe that thou art the Christ, the Son of God, which should come into the world.**

Verse 27 is Martha's response to Jesus' question at the end of verse 26. Bible commentators disagree about the adequacy of Martha's confession of faith. Some feel that she missed the point of Jesus' words in verses 25-26. They base this view on the fact that Martha later objected to Jesus' order to roll the stone away from the tomb of Lazarus (see v. 39). Other Bible commentators believe that verse 27 expresses a strong confession of faith in light of the revelation she had received at the time. She may not have understood all the implications of Jesus' great claim in verses 25-26, but neither had the twelve and His other followers.

Martha used many of the same words that Peter used in his great confession at Caesarea Philippi in Matthew 16:16. Jesus commended Peter for that confession, even though Peter did not understand the prediction by Jesus of His coming death and resurrection. Martha confessed that she believed (**I believe**) that Jesus is **the Christ, the Son of God, which should come into the world.** This was an expression of genuine faith, based on the revelation Martha had at the time. These words show Martha to have been a woman of deep faith, in spite of the fact that some see her as less spiritual because of the account in Luke 10:38-42.

Human faith is a response to the revelation of God. Our faith is not perfect, but God accepts sincere faith that is based on the revelation we have received. After the death and resurrection of Jesus, believers were able to confess Jesus as their crucified and risen Savior and Lord.

Demonstration of Power (John 11:38-45)

In what way was Jesus deeply moved as He came near the tomb of Lazarus? What is the significance of Martha's objection to opening the tomb? Why does faith enable us to **see the glory of God**? What was the purpose of Jesus' prayer? How did people respond to Lazarus's resurrection? Of what is this miracle a sign? These questions are addressed in comments on verses 38-45.

Verse 38: **Jesus therefore again groaning in himself cometh to the grave. It was a cave, and a stone lay upon it.**

The words **again groaning in himself** ("once more deeply moved," NIV) call for some comments on verses 28-37. Jesus called Mary to come to where He waited outside the village, and Mary immediately went. The mourners in the house followed her, thinking she was going to the tomb. The custom of the day was for friends and sometimes paid mourners to weep with the bereaved family during their time of sorrow (vv. 28-31). When she saw Jesus, she made the same comment that Martha had made in verse 21 (v. 32). Jesus saw Mary and the mourners weeping, and "he was deeply moved in spirit and troubled" (v. 33, NIV). When He asked where the burial place of Lazarus was, they said, "Come and see" (v. 34). When "Jesus wept" (v. 35), the mourners saw this as evidence of Jesus' love for Lazarus (v. 36). They wondered whether He who opened the eyes of the man born blind (see 9:1-41) could also have healed Lazarus (v. 37).

Groaning is the word *embrimomenos.* Translators struggle to find the right English word to translate it. The Greek word refers to deep emotion, usually anger. This emotion often is expressed in sounds. This is an old Greek verb that originally referred to the snorting of a horse. It is found three other times in the New Testament. A. T. Robertson wrote: "The notion of indignation is present in the other examples of the word in the N. T. (Mark 1:43; 14:5; Matt. 9:30). So it seems best to see that sense here."[3] Other commentators think that the word here only shows sounds resulting from deep emotions.

Assuming that the word indicates some anger, about what would Jesus have been angry? And how does this fit the fact that "Jesus wept" (v. 35)? If Jesus was angry, His anger probably was directed against the enemy of death and the hopeless sounds of the weeping He heard from the mourners. When Jesus went to Jairus's house, He threw the professional mourners out because their mourning was superficial (Mark 5:38-40). Jesus own weeping is indicated by a different Greek word (*edakrusen*) than that used of the mourners (*klaiontas*). The word *edakrusen* indicates shedding tears but not wailing. Jesus obviously was deeply moved by what was happening. He may have felt a mixture of anger and grief. There is no doubt that He entered into the genuine grief of the two sisters.

The grave was **a cave, and a stone lay upon it.** Some graves had an opening on top; others had an opening on the side. The Greek preposition *epi* **(upon)** can mean "on" or "against." Thus this **cave** may have been of either type. The **stone** was intended to keep out intruders.

Verse 39: **Jesus said, Take ye away the stone. Martha, the sister of him that was dead, saith unto him, Lord, by this time he stinketh: for he hath been dead four days.**

When **Jesus** gave orders to move **the stone, Martha** objected. When someone died in that day in Palestine, the deceased was buried as soon as possible. Although spices were used, the Jews did not have an embalming process as did the Egyptians. Therefore, because Lazarus had **been dead four days,** his body had no doubt begun to decay. Martha did not want to let loose the bad odors that were present after four days.

Some Bible students see this objection as evidence that Martha's earlier expressions of faith (vv. 24,27) were lacking the elements of true faith. But is it fair to expect Martha to know what Jesus intended to do? She had no reason to expect Jesus to call her brother back from the dead. She had not seen all the implications of Jesus' words in verses 25-26, but neither had anyone else. Her reaction, therefore, was a natural concern of a sister for a beloved brother.

Verse 40: **Jesus saith unto her, Said I not unto thee, that, if thou wouldest believe, thou shouldest see the glory of God?**

Jesus' words in verse 40 may be taken as a mild rebuke or they can be seen as a reminder that faith is necessary to see **the glory of God.** Jesus had told His disciples that the ultimate result of the death of Lazarus would be the glory of God (v. 4). Only believers saw **the glory of God** in Jesus' sign-miracles. Others may have seen the same things; but unless they looked through the eyes of faith, they failed to see the divine reality in the event. According to verse 45, some believed as a result of seeing the raising of Lazarus through eyes of faith; others saw the same things, but they did not believe (v. 46).

Verses 41-45: **Then they took away the stone from the place where the dead was laid. And Jesus lifted up his eyes, and said, Father, I thank thee that thou hast heard me.** [42]**And I knew that thou hearest me always: but because of the people which stand by I said it, that they may believe that thou hast sent me.** [43]**And when he thus had spoken, he cried with a loud voice, Lazarus, come forth.** [44]**And he that was dead came forth, bound hand and foot with graveclothes: and his face was bound about with a napkin. Jesus saith unto them, Loose him, and let him go.** [45]**Then many of** the Jews which came to Mary, and had seen the things which Jesus did, believed on him.

We do not know who **they** were that **took away the stone.** Perhaps they were the disciples or people who had come to comfort the grieving sisters. Jesus then thanked His **Father** for hearing His prayer. He expressed confidence that the Father **always** heard Him. Jesus said that He spoke this prayer **because of the people which stand by.** He wanted them to **believe that** God had **sent** Him.

Then Jesus **cried with a loud voice, Lazarus, come forth.** The loud voice may have been so that all would hear. Jesus knew Lazarus, and He called him by name. Some have suggested that if Jesus had not used Lazarus's name, all the dead in that area would have come forth. Lazarus **came forth, bound hand and foot with graveclothes.** The custom of the day was to wrap the body with cloths. **Jesus** told those who were there: **Loose him, and let him go.**

The responses of the witnesses to this remarkable miracle varied. Verse 45 focuses on those who **believed on him.** This was Jesus' hope for all those who **had seen the things which Jesus did.** Others who had witnessed the same sign-miracle reported these things to the enemies of Jesus, who were seeking His death (v. 46). Their report led the religious leaders to meet together and plot the death of Jesus (vv. 47-54). Miracles do not force faith; some who see miracles turn away from the truth of what they have seen.

What is the message of this miraculous sign? For one thing, people in sin are as hopelessly dead in their sins as a person who has been dead physically for four days. For another, Jesus is able to raise the spiritually dead to new life even as He can raise the physically dead. And still another, Jesus is able to give eternal life that extends beyond death.

Jesus is able to save those who seem hopelessly dead in their sins. Robert McAfee Brown, a chaplain, was on a troop ship returning to America from Japan. He was glad to see a number of military personnel at the Bible study sessions. One session included John 11. After the session, a young marine said something like this to the chaplain: "Everything in that story we have been studying today points to me. I've been in hell for the last six months; and since I have heard this chapter I am just getting free." The young man went on to confess the serious trouble he had gotten himself into. No one but God knew about it. He had a deep sense of guilt. He had felt that his life was ruined. He added: "I've been a dead man . . . but after reading this chapter I'm alive again. . . . This Resurrection and Life that Jesus was talking about is the real thing here and now." The man who felt like a dead man because of his sins, Jesus brought to life again. Jesus raised him to new life.[4]

Jesus also promises eternal, resurrection life for believers. His victory over death enables Him to assure us that death is dead and that He will raise us up at the last day.

We wonder what happened to Lazarus. The only thing the Bible tells us is that he later was at a meal with Jesus, Jesus' disciples, Martha, and Mary (12:1-9). One old legend says that Lazarus never smiled again. I prefer Eugene O'Neill's imaginative depiction in a play called "Lazarus Laughed." O'Neill imagined a Lazarus who saw life through the eyes of one who had been on both sides of death. He laughed at the values of people who lived only for this life or at people who feared death. After his encounter with death, Lazarus said: "Laugh! Laugh with me! Death is dead! Fear is no more! There is only life! There is only laughter!"[5]

❖ Spiritual Transformations

Martha expressed regret that Jesus had not arrived in time to heal Lazarus, but she expressed faith in prayer and hope of the future resurrection. Jesus asked Martha if she believed that He gives life that begins with faith and extends beyond death. Martha confessed faith that Jesus is the Messiah and the Son of God. Jesus raised Lazarus from the dead, although he had been dead for four days.

People of faith pray with honesty, faith, and hope. Jesus is the resurrection and the life, who promised that believers are alive beyond death and that believers will be raised from the death at the end of time. Christians believe that Jesus is the resurrection and the life. Jesus can raise the worst of sinners to new life now, and He gives hope to believers when they are dying or bereaved.

How do you feel about the statement that a person is not ready to live until that person is ready to die? _____

In what kinds of situations has this Bible passage been meaningful to you? __

Prayer of Commitment: O Lord, the resurrection and the life, help me to live in light of who You are.

[1]Borchert, "John," NAC, 355.

[2]Herschel H. Hobbs, *The Gospel of John: Invitation to Life* [Nashville: Convention Press, 1988], 70.

[3]A. T. Robertson, *Word Pictures in the New Testament,* vol. 5 [Nashville: Broadman Press, 1932], 202.

[4]Quoted by William Barclay, *And He Had Compassion on Them,* 228-229.

[5]Eugene O'Neill, "Lazarus Laughed," in *The Plays of Eugene O'Neill,* vol. 3 [New York: The Modern Library, 1974], 280.

ESTABLISHING LIFE'S PRIORITY

Bible Passage: Mark 10:17-31
Key Verse: Mark 10:28

❖ *Significance of the Lesson*

• The *Theme* of this lesson is that nothing should take priority over Jesus in a person's life.

• The *Life Question* this lesson seeks to address is Who or what should have priority in my life?

• The *Biblical Theme* is that Jesus demands that people give Him priority in their lives.

• The *Life Impact* is to help you give Jesus priority in your life.

What Are Priorities?

The English word *priorities* comes from Latin words meaning "before," "former," or "superior." It means something that is before other things in time or importance. The English word *priorities* is seldom used in translations of the Bible, but the concept is expressed in many Bible superlatives: "first," "greatest," "all," "highest," and "most." Priorities are things for which we seek first, in which we place our greatest trust, to which we give our highest devotion, and on which we spend most of our resources. People often claim to have one set of priorities, but their actions reveal their true priorities.

Adults and Their Priorities

In a secular worldview, priorities center around self rather than God and others. Those who follow self-centered priorities seek success as defined by the world. Success and security are measured most often by possessions, power, and pleasures.

In the biblical worldview, God and others are priorities. Following Jesus by denying self takes priority. Success is measured by the standards of God's eternal kingdom. True security is found only in a right relationship with the Lord.

The Rich Young Ruler

The encounter of Jesus with the rich young ruler is recorded in all three Synoptic Gospels (Matt. 19:16-30; Mark 10:17-31; Luke 18:18-30). All three note the man was wealthy. Matthew 19:20 calls him "young." Luke 18:18 calls him a "ruler." The word for "ruler" is *archon*, which was used of a ruler in a synagogue (Jairus in Luke 8:41), a member of the Sanhedrin (Nicodemus in John 3:1), and a government official (Rom. 13:3). We do not know what kind of ruler this man was, but his young age shows that he had received wealth and power earlier than most of his day.

Word Study: *Inherit*

According to Mark 10:17, the rich young ruler asked Jesus what he needed to do to **inherit eternal life.** The word translated **inherit** is *kleronomeo*, which at times has the specific meaning of "inherit" and at other times has a more general meaning of "acquire" or "receive." The same word was spoken by the lawyer in Luke 10:25. The *King James Version*, along with most modern translations, use **inherit.** The *Good News Bible: Today's English Version* reads "to receive eternal life." Possibly the man meant "inherit" since a different word for "receive" (*lambano*) is used in connection with "eternal life" when Jesus spoke to His disciples in verse 30. On the other hand, perhaps this shows that the words could be used interchangeably. *Which meaning do you think the rich young ruler intended? On what basis have you made your decision?*

❖ *Search the Scriptures*

When the rich young ruler asked about inheriting eternal life, Jesus told him to sell all he had and follow Him. The man went away because of his great wealth. When Jesus told His disciples how hard it is for a rich man to enter the kingdom, they were astonished and asked who could be saved. Jesus told them that salvation is not possible through human efforts; it is an act of God. When Peter asked what the disciples would receive for leaving all to follow Him, Jesus assured them of rewards but added that the first would be last and the last would be first.

A Difficult Demand (Mark 10:17-22)

Why did the rich man come to Jesus? Why did Jesus question his use of the word **good**? Why did Jesus make such a difficult demand on the man? Why did the man fail to follow Jesus? Why did Jesus let him go away? What do these verses teach about priorities? These questions are addressed in the comments on these verses.

Verses 17-20: And when he was gone forth into the way, there came one running, and kneeled to him, and asked him, Good Master, what shall I do that I may inherit eternal life? [18]And Jesus said unto him, Why callest thou me good? there is none good but one, that is, God. [19]Thou knowest the commandments, Do not commit adultery, Do not kill, Do not steal, Do not bear false witness, Defraud not, Honor thy father and mother. [20]And he answered and said unto him, Master, all these have I observed from my youth.

The mention of Jesus continuing **into the way** refers to His journey to Jerusalem and the cross. The repetition of His prediction in verses 32-34 begins "and they were in the way going up to Jerusalem."

The words **running** and **kneeled** show the sincerity and earnestness of the rich young ruler. He asked the same question as the lawyer in Luke 10:25, but he had no ulterior motive in asking the question (as the lawyer did). Apparently he sincerely was seeking an answer to the most important issue for any person—**eternal life.** The young man came asking about eternal life, which surely ought to be the priority of all people. Nothing is more important than **eternal life,** as defined in the Bible. "And this is life eternal," Jesus said in a prayer, "that they might know thee the only true God, and Jesus Christ whom thou hast sent" (John 17:3). To **inherit eternal life** is used interchangeably with to **receive . . . eternal life** in verse 30, to **enter into the kingdom of God** (vv. 23-24), and to **be saved** in verse 26.

The young man addressed Jesus as **Good Master** ("Good teacher," NIV, HCSB). Jesus asked him **why** he called Him **good.** Jesus' explanation for His question was, **There is none good but one, that is, God.** Jesus' answer has been greatly misused and misunderstood by people who interpret it to mean that Jesus was denying His own goodness and deity. Actually, the words are an affirmation of both, while at the same time probing the man's definition of **good.** Notice that "Jesus does not say 'I am not good.' He says: 'Why do you call me good? Goodness exists only in God.' That is, are your words only a conventional flattery or do you perceive that my goodness can have only one source, God?"[1]

Jesus was not denying His goodness or His deity. Both His sinlessness (Heb. 4:15; 1 Pet. 2:22) and His deity (Mark 1:1; John 1:1) are affirmed in the New Testament. And here too Jesus was affirming them. At the same time, He was suggesting that the rich young ruler's question revealed a superficial understanding of what is **good.** The fact that the man asked, "What good thing must I do, that I may have eternal life?" (Matt. 19:16) indicates that "the inquirer's idea of goodness was defined by human achievement. He undoubtedly regarded himself as 'good.'"[2] He thought he could learn the "good thing," and he thought he could **do** it.

This is confirmed by verses 19-20. Jesus concentrated on the last six of the Ten Commandments, which have to do with relations with other people. The Fifth through the Ninth Commandments are easily recognized, even though they are not in the usual sequence: **Do not commit adultery, Do not kill, Do not steal, Do not bear false witness . . . Honor thy father and mother. Defraud not** is not the wording of the Tenth Commandment, but it may reflect that Commandment.

Why did Jesus ask about the man's obedience to these Commandments? It certainly was not because He believed that salvation comes by keeping the Law. Perhaps Jesus hoped to find some sense of humility and spiritual need in the man. However, the man quickly claimed, **All these have I observed from my youth** ("since I was a boy," NIV). He obviously had not heard Jesus' inward interpretation of some of these Commandments in Matthew 5:21-48. If he had, he may not have been so quick to claim to have kept these Commandments!

Verse 21: **Then Jesus beholding him loved him, and said unto him, One thing thou lackest: go thy way, sell whatsoever thou hast, and give to the poor, and thou shalt have treasure in heaven: and come, take up the cross, and follow me.**

One of the unique things in Mark's account of the encounter of Jesus and the rich young ruler are the words, **Jesus beholding him loved him.** Of course, Jesus loved all people, but He especially had love for this young man, who was so close yet so far from the eternal life he sought.

Because Jesus loved him, He told him what was needed to receive the eternal life He sought and which he so desperately needed. The man's need is reflected in the words, **One thing thou lackest.** Matthew 19:20 says that Jesus was answering the young man's question, "What lack I yet?" Picking up on this question, Jesus focused on the one thing he needed in order to have eternal life.

The rich young ruler was concerned about what ought to be a priority of all people—**eternal life.** Unfortunately, he had the wrong idea about how to receive it. Perhaps he felt that he already had it based on his striving to live a good life. Perhaps he also felt that his wealth confirmed God's favor on him. Possibly he came to Jesus just to receive reassurance that he had eternal life, or to hear Jesus tell him of one other good thing he might do to ensure it. Thus he asked, "What lack I yet?" Or perhaps the ruler's question pointed to a deep lack he still felt in his life even after he tried to do all that the Law demanded.

The rich young ruler must have been surprised by the high demands Jesus made of him. Jesus said that he must **sell** everything he possessed, **give** it **to the poor,** and then he was to **come . . . and follow** Jesus. (The words **take up thy cross** are not in the oldest copies of v. 21. For this reason they do not appear in the *New International Version* or in the *Holman Christian Standard Bible.* Neither are they in the parallel accounts in Matthew and Luke. They are found, however, in Jesus' call to discipleship in Mark 8:34. Thus we could say that they are implied in what Jesus said here.)

We have two questions about this demand: (1) Why did Jesus make it of the rich young ruler? (2) Does Jesus make the same demand of all who follow Him? Jesus did not explain why He made such a demand of this man, but the answer seems to be that the man was trusting in his possessions as his basis for confidence of God's favor in this life and his assurance of acceptance into the life to come. Jesus knew that great possessions do not ensure eternal life. In fact, He went on to teach that rich men have difficulty in entering the kingdom (vv. 23-25). Notice that Jesus did not mention the first four Commandments in verse 19, which deal with a right relation with God. The rich man's problem lay in this area, although he probably did not recognize that he had substituted mammon for God. Jesus taught that we cannot serve God and mammon (Matt. 6:24). The man's trust in his riches was the barrier between himself and God. Only as he surrendered what he most loved could he fully trust in God, whom to know is life eternal.

The answer to the second question is both yes and no. No, Jesus does not demand that each person sell all his or her possessions and give them to the poor. Yes, Jesus does demand that each follower deny self, take up the cross, and follow Him. This means to turn from any false trusts and commit ourselves totally to the Lord. For most people, this does not mean selling all we possess and giving it to the poor. But He does demand that we do whatever is necessary to seek first the kingdom of God and then trust Him to provide for our needs (Matt. 6:25-34).

The principle Jesus used in calling this man to repentance and faith was to press him at the point of his resistance to the gospel. That is a valid principle. If a person surrenders to Christ at the point of his greatest resistance, the person usually is saved because surrender at that point leads to total surrender of life.

Verse 22: **And he was sad at that saying, and went away grieved: for he had great possessions.**

The rich young ruler now faced the most important decision of his life. It was a decision only he could make. Jesus yearned for him to make the right decision, but Jesus did not force him. The Bible does not use the word "surprised" to describe the man's feelings; it uses **sad** and **grieved.** The word rendered **sad** (*stugnasas*) means "to become gloomy," as a lowering cloud (see Matt. 16:3, "the sky is red and lowring"). You can just see the man's face drop when he heard Jesus' words. The *New International Version* reads "the man's face fell." His whole countenance fell! The *Holman Christian Standard Bible* renders it "he was stunned at this demand." The word **grieved** (*lupoumenos*) is a present participle—"he went away grieving" (HCSB). He was "sorrowful" (NKJV). The ruler had these feelings because he decided to go away rather than to follow Jesus. The Bible tells us that he made this decision because **he had great possessions.** The rich young ruler was not willing to give up these possessions. They were the basis for his trust and the foundation of his security for the future. They were his true priorities.

In one of the paintings of this dramatic moment, the artist pictures Jesus looking with concern toward the well-dressed young man. The rich man is pondering his decision. When he decided, he went away; and Jesus let him go away. Why didn't Jesus stop him? He didn't stop him for the same reason that the father of the prodigal son did not stop his son from going to the far country. God created people free to choose to serve God or not to serve Him.

Thus the rich young ruler came to Jesus about what should be the greatest priority of all of us—**eternal life**; however, when he learned that he must give up his true priority—his wealth—he refused. This is life's greatest tragedy—to refuse to follow Jesus and receive eternal life. Possessions often are the barrier between people and God. The Gospels tell of other rich men who missed eternal life. The rich man of Luke 12:16-21 was too preoccupied with possessions to have time for God or others. The rich man in Luke 16:19-31 went to hell because his wealth made him indifferent to God and to the needs of a beggar at his gate. The rich young ruler was not guilty of such sins—at least nothing is said about such sins as exploiting others, ignoring the needy, or being too preoccupied with things to ask about eternal life. This man probably gave some alms to the poor; what he refused to do was to give everything to them.

Of course, preoccupation with possessions and wealth is not confined to the wealthy. James 4:14-16 tells of merchants who presumed that they would always be alive and able to transact business. Matthew 6:25-34 tells of poor people who are anxious about food and clothing to survive. Jesus told them to seek first God's kingdom (Matt. 6:33). If they made this their priority, they could trust the Father to supply their needs. And we already have studied in a previous lesson Jesus' parable of the sower and the soils. There we learned that many let "the cares of this world," the "pleasures of this life," "the lusts of other things," and "the deceitfulness of riches" choke out the seed of God's Word (Matt. 13:22; Mark 4:19; Luke 8:14).

A Divine Accomplishment (Mark 10:23-27)

Why did Jesus say that it is so hard for a rich person to enter the kingdom of God? Why were the disciples surprised at this teaching? How is salvation possible? These questions are addressed in the comments on these verses.

Verses 23-25: **And Jesus looked round about, and saith unto his disciples, How hardly shall they that have riches enter into the kingdom of God! 24And the disciples were astonished at his words. But Jesus answereth again, and saith unto them, Children, how hard is it for them that trust in riches to enter into the kingdom of God! 25It is easier for a camel to go through the eye of a needle, than for a rich man to enter into the kingdom of God. 26And they were astonished out of measure, saying among themselves, Who then can be saved? 27And Jesus looking upon them saith, With men it is impossible, but not with God: for with God all things are possible.**

Hardly translates *duskolos,* which means "how hard" (NIV) or "how difficult" it is. Jesus used the same word again in verse 24. **Riches** translates *chremata,* which means "property," "wealth," or "means." This is a different word from *plousios,* **a rich man** in verse 25. *Chremata* can mean "money," but it often means "things" or "possessions." Many people do not think of themselves as **rich,** but they have many possessions, which take priority in their lives—getting them, enjoying them, keeping them.

Why were the disciples **astonished** at Jesus' words? We see from verse 26 that the disciples shared the view of many people of their day—that wealth is a sure sign of God's favor. Not only is wealth not a guarantee of God's favor but it also can be what keeps people from God. Have we learned this lesson? Many people in our materialistic society stand in awe of the rich. If the disciples had been in charge of accepting new disciples, the rich young ruler surely would have been warmly accepted. They may have been like the church members of James 2:1-8, who fawned over a rich visitor and ignored a poor visitor. They thought of what the rich man could do for their church. What kind of people do we consider our best prospects? Do we rank people by their needs or by what they can give?

Jesus added to the disciples' astonishment by making His point even more strongly. Jesus said that **it is easier for a camel to go through the eye of a needle, than for a rich man to enter into the kingdom of God.** Some Bible students try to weaken this saying by identifying **the eye of a needle** with a narrow gate into Jerusalem that a camel could squeeze through by stooping; however, there was no such gate. By means of an eastern proverb, Jesus expressed the *impossible,* not the *possible*—as He stated directly in verse 27. A **camel** cannot go through **the eye of a needle.** Mark and Matthew used the word for an ordinary **needle** (*rhaphidos*). Luke, reflecting his medical background, used the word for a surgical needle (*belone,* 18:25; the only time this word is used in the New Testament).

We must remember that this saying of verse 25 is an expansion of Jesus' sayings in verses 23 and 24. In verse 23 Jesus clearly exclaimed, "How hard it is for the rich to enter the kingdom of God!" (NIV). In verse 24 Jesus expanded, not merely repeated, that judgment—"Children, how hard it is to enter the kingdom of God!" (NIV). The words **for them that trust in riches,** in verse 24, are not in the oldest copies of Mark's Gospel and therefore do not appear in the *New International Version* or in the *Holman Christian Standard Bible.* Thus in verse 24 Jesus applied the principle to all people, not just to the rich. It is impossible for *any* person to enter the kingdom of God based on who he or she is, what he or she has, or what he or she does.

This caused the disciples to be **astonished out of measure** ("even more amazed," NIV). It led to the disciples' question, **Who then can be saved?** If it's that difficult to enter the kingdom of God, who can? If a rich person can't be saved, who can be? Don't Jesus' sayings make it impossible for anyone to enter the kingdom of God? Jesus Himself drew the conclusion— **With men it is impossible** ("With people it is impossible," NASB). **It** refers to entering the kingdom, receiving eternal life, and being saved. People cannot be saved based on anything they have or do—whether they are rich or not. This is true of those who trust in their own goodness or anything else.

If Jesus had ended with the words **with men it is impossible,** the disciples—and indeed all human beings—would have been left in despair. But Jesus added, **but not with God: for with God all things are possible.** "Salvation is completely beyond the sphere of human possibilities; every attempt to enter the Kingdom on the basis of achievement or merit is futile. Yet even the rule of the impossibility of entrance into the Kingdom for the rich is limited by the sovereign action of God himself. The ability and the power to effect deliverance reside in God alone (cf. Rom. 8:7). 'Eternal life,' 'salvation,' or 'entrance into the Kingdom' describe a single reality which must be bestowed as his gift to men. The conclusion to the account rejoins the beginning in directing attention to the ability and goodness of God."[3]

To be **saved** assumes that the person being saved is being rescued from a deadly plight from which he or she cannot save himself or herself. Suppose a person was drowning and unable to make it to shore and safety. A life guard comes to save or rescue the drowning person. If the drowning person wants to be rescued, the person needs to surrender to the life guard in order for the life guard to be able to swim to safety holding the person's mouth and nose above the water. If the drowning person tries to assist by grabbing the life guard, both may end up being drowned. Sinners are perishing in their sins. Jesus is the Savior. Only as people trust completely in Him can they be saved. Trying to save ourselves or helping to save ourselves will not result in salvation. Nothing we do can save us from sin; only by trusting Jesus can anyone be saved. Salvation is a divine accomplishment.

A Disproportionate Reward (Mark 10:28-31)

What does Peter's question reveal? What did Jesus mean by referring to a **hundredfold** reward? How can persecution be part of a reward? What is the meaning of verse 31?

Verses 28-31: **Then Peter began to say unto him, Lo, we have left all, and have followed thee.** [29]**And Jesus answered and said, Verily I say unto you, There is no man that hath left house, or brethren, or sisters, or father, or mother, or wife, or children, or lands, for my sake, and the gospel's,** [30]**but he shall receive an hundredfold now in this time, houses, and brethren, and sisters, and mothers, and children, and lands, with persecutions; and in the world to come eternal life.** [31]**But many that are first shall be last; and the last first.**

Peter, as usual, put the disciples' thoughts into words. He reminded Jesus that they had done what the rich young ruler had refused to do—**left all, and have followed thee.** Matthew 19:27 says that Peter's comment concluded with the question, "what shall we have therefore?" This is implicit in the statement as recorded by Mark. Peter boldly asked about their rewards for forsaking all and following Jesus.

Jesus responded to Peter in four ways. (1) He said there will be rewards for following Him. He indicated that these rewards will be far more than anything given up for His sake. He addressed His promise to anyone who **left house, or brethren, or sisters, or father, or mother, or wife, or children, or lands, for my sake, and the gospel's.** Jesus promised that such sacrifices would be rewarded **an hundredfold now in this time, houses, and brethren, and sisters, and mothers, and children, and lands.** The word **wife** in verse 29 is not in the oldest copies of Mark. Hence, it does not appear in the *New International Version* or in the *Holman Christian Standard Bible.* How literally can we take this promise? We can take it literally if we do so in light of Jesus' description of the extended family, who constitute the family of believers in the Heavenly Father (see 3:33-35). Jesus was saying that the rewards of following Him are disproportionate to anything given up in order to follow Him.

(2) He said there would be **persecutions.** This was also part of the legacy of Jesus. His followers would endure persecution for Jesus' sake and for the gospel's. Yet He promised that even persecution for His sake is blessed (Matt. 5:10-12). This was literally true for these hearers. It has been true for many of Jesus' followers throughout the centuries. And it is true today for many believers around the world.

(3) He said they would **receive . . . in the world to come eternal life.** This is not a reward for their faithfulness but a gift of God's grace. True disciples are willing to give their lives for Christ. As Jesus promised in 8:35—by losing our lives for His sake and the gospel's, we find life.

(4) He said that **many that are first shall be last; and the last first.** This is part of Jesus' answer to Peter's question—perhaps the most important part. But what is the meaning of this enigmatic promise? The story of the laborers in the vineyard in Matthew 20:1-16 was a parable that Jesus told to shed light on this strange statement when He used it in another context (see v. 16). One of the main points of the parable is that although rewards are real, they are not based on what we have done but on the grace of God. God's rewards are actually gifts of His grace. Thus Jesus' response to Peter's question reassured him and the others that the rewards will be real and generous, but they are not so much rewards as gifts of grace.

Another truth in verse 31 concerns the surprises of the rewards and judgment. Those who expect to be **first** will be **last** and those who expect to be **last** will be **first.** Jesus illustrated this in Matthew 25:31-46 and Luke 18:10-14.

The disciples had not learned this lesson. Their ongoing debate among themselves was which of them was the greatest. Shortly after the events and teachings of Mark 10:17-31, Jesus again predicted His death and resurrection. Their failure to understand is seen in James's and John's request to have the chief places in the coming kingdom and the anger of the other disciples that the brothers had sought the places they wanted for themselves. Jesus patiently taught them once again that greatness in God's kingdom is based on humble service, not on power and position (vv. 35-45).

> The world, I thought, belonged to me,
>> Goods, gold, and people, land, and sea.
> Where'er I walked beneath God's sky,
>> In those old days, my word was "I."

Years passed: there flashed my pathway near,
  The fragment of a vision dear;
My former word no more sufficed,
  And what I said was "I and Christ."
But, O, the more I looked on Him,
  His glory grew, while mine grew dim;
I shrank so small, He towered so high,
  All I dared say was "Christ and I."
Years more the vision held its place
  And looked me steadily in the face;
I speak now in a humbler tone,
  And what I say is "Christ alone!"[4]

❖ *Spiritual Transformations*

The rich young ruler came to ask what he could do to inherit eternal life. When Jesus told him to sell his possessions, give the proceeds to the poor, and follow Him, the young man went away because he was unwilling to do what Jesus demanded. When Jesus said that it was impossible for a rich man to enter the kingdom, the disciples were amazed. Jesus then told them that no one can save himself, but that God is able to save anyone who trusts in Him. When Peter asked about the disciples' rewards, Jesus taught them that their rewards will be real but gifts of grace.

Priorities take first place in our lives. They are the things in which we trust and to which we give our devotion. Possessions are priorities in many people's lives. Yet possessions cannot save; indeed, they can become gods that fill the first place in our lives, into which only God rightly will fit.

What are your priorities? _____

On what do you spend most of your resources: time, energy, talents? _____
_____

In what do you place your trust for life here and hereafter? _____
_____

Prayer of Commitment: Lord, help me to seek first Your kingdom and righteousness.

[1]A. M. Hunter, *The Gospel According to Saint Mark,* 102.
[2]William L. Lane, *The Gospel According to Mark,* in The New International Commentary on the New Testament [Grand Rapids: William B. Eerdmans Publishing Company, 1974], 365.
[3]Lane, *The Gospel According to Mark,* 370.
[4]"Christ Alone," quoted in Zuck, *The Speaker's Quote Book,* 58.